CHERIE

The Perfect Life
of
Mrs Blair

CHERIE

The Perfect Life of Mrs Blair

Linda McDougall

First published in Great Britain 2001
by Politico's Publishing
8 Artillery Row
Westminster
London
SW1P 1RZ

Tel 020 7931 0090
Fax 020 7828 8111
Email publishing@politicos.co.uk
Website http://www.politicos.co.uk/publishing

First published in hardback 2001

A catalogue record of this book is available from the British Library.

ISBN 1 902301 87 0

Printed and bound in Great Britain by Creative Print and Design.

Contents

Acknowledgements

Being thanked by me could well be the kiss of death for a Westminster politician or journalist so I have avoided the risk and refrained from thanking some of the people who helped me most.

The journalist Susan Crosland generously gave me transcripts of her unpublished interviews with Lord Irvine and Lord Falconer, Maggie Rae and Michael Beloff. She, too, had tried to write a profile of Cherie but gave up when an interview with Cherie was refused by Alastair Campbell. As well as being a distinguished journalist and biographer, Susan Crosland is the widow of Anthony Crosland, Labour Foreign Secretary in the 1970s. Susan and I share an important historical connection. Both of us have been happily married to Members of Parliament for Grimsby. Maybe there's something in the water.

Tom Pollock, Rachael Webb, Andi d'Sa and Olivia Bellers made the film *The Real Cherie Booth* for Channel 4. David Lloyd and Caroline Haydon commissioned it. All these people shared with me a healthy enthusiasm to know more about Cherie and I am very grateful to them.

Ian Bloom gave me valuable support and encouragement whenever the project seemed wobbly, and wise advice when it flourished.

I couldn't have managed without my editor Catherine Hurley and Sean Magee, John Berry and Iain Dale at Politico's. They turned my enthusiastic efforts into a book.

Susan, Jonathan and Hannah Mitchell continued to listen patiently to my stories about Cherie long after the politest non-family member had packed up and gone.

And finally my husband Austin Mitchell discussed ideas with

me, read chapters, and came up with brilliant suggestions for improvements, while sitting at our kitchen table waiting for me to cook his dinner.

Introduction
DESPERATELY
SEEKING CHERIE

When Tony Blair won the General Election in 1997, it was the beginning of a new era. After eighteen years of Conservative government everything felt fresh and different. The new Prime Minister was the youngest for over a hundred years and he had a young family. Tony Blair moved into Downing Street with his wife and three children. There hadn't been children in Downing Street for decades and Mrs Blair was the first ever Prime Minister's wife to be a working mum. Cherie Booth QC had a professional life of her own as a barrister specializing in employment and human rights law.

Women like me, who had worked all their lives while running a home and bringing up their families, celebrated the arrival of Cherie as a second victory for New Labour. It was as if at long last working mums had been given the official seal of approval. Like many other working women I felt this was the best change of all.

I was fascinated by Cherie. Where did she come from, how had she managed it? How had she succeeded in persuading her husband that responsibility for the family was something to be shared fifty-fifty and not simply piled on top of the wife's professional commitments? We knew she had achieved the breakthrough, because the new Prime Minister frequently spoke of his commitment to caring for his family as the most important work in his life.

When I spoke occasionally to women's groups outside London about my life as a Westminster wife, I was always asked more questions about Cherie than about any Westminster politician.

Because I wanted to know more about Cherie and felt that other people did too, the idea of a biography was born.

Who was this woman who not only seemed to be succeeding in everything she had taken on, but was the person closest to our new Prime Minister? I believed there was genuine public interest, and there is even more today, now that Cherie has added to her responsibilities by producing Leo Blair, and by taking on her husband's government in several high-profile court cases.

I wrote to Cherie to tell her of my plans and to ask her if she would co-operate. I got a letter back from her aide Fiona Millar. In essence it said that Cherie did not want her biography written and she planned to tell her friends not to co-operate with me.

I was disappointed but not surprised. Downing Street, and the machine which runs it sees everyone outside a tiny closed circle as the enemy. It will probably puzzle readers who have no experience of professional politics that although my husband Austin Mitchell has been a loyal Labour Member of Parliament for over twenty years, we are regarded as outsiders who are not to be trusted and have little to do with Tony Blair's Government. With a huge majority in its second term the gap between the Government and the backbench Members of Parliament who support it has never been wider.

It also didn't matter how many times I explained to Downing Street that I was a fan of Cherie, that my aim was not to search for scandal but to write her life story: I continued to get a negative response. Dozens of people at Westminster expressed their sympathy for the impossibility of my task. Many of them said that they too would like to know more about Cherie but wouldn't dare to take on the job. They had careers in front of them and could not risk them being ruined. This may sound melodramatic, but ask the political correspondent of your local

TV station or newspaper what they think would happen to them if they wrote something critical of the Downing Street machine or tried to find out about the personal life of the Blairs. That sort of behaviour is punishable by exclusion and it's impossible to work as a journalist at Westminster if you don't get any co-operation from the people running the show.

Yet I decided to go ahead with my quest to find out more about Mrs Blair.

In their attempt to keep as much power in their own hands as possible, both Blairs turn their relationships with ordinary people on and off like a tap. At election time they will be down your street or in your community centre exposing as much of themselves as they need to get your vote. Of course politicians of every shade have always done that. The most common complaint of constituents is that 'we only ever see you at election time', but the Blairs have turned this kind of behaviour into high art. They will chat to you about baby Leo's first steps or confide that Kathryn has just passed her grade 5 piano exam, but as soon as the election is over you will be told that the children's privacy must be protected at all costs. The moat has been filled for the next five years, the tap has been turned off and the Blairs retreat to the safety of their holiday castle or Downing Street stockade.

Cherie will now be silent again for another four years and her husband will give us occasional little lectures sadly implying that as an electorate we don't really live up to his hopes for us. He will tell us it is policies not personalities we should be interested in. But being interested in personalities is human nature, and wanting to know more about Tony Blair or Cherie Booth is hardly surprising, when he's running the country, and she's his influential other half.

During the year I have been working on this biography of Cherie Booth I have approached just about everyone who is close to or has been close to, Cherie. I phoned. I emailed. I wrote. Most people either ignored me completely or wrote to say that they would love to help but they didn't want to be disloyal to Cherie. All those I spoke to admired her enormously. She inspired a loyalty in her friends and colleagues that would humble lesser mortals. Just a few people agreed to talk to me 'off-the-record' about their good friend Cherie. A few more brave souls spoke out publicly.

So putting this biography together was pioneering work. I started and ended up as an admirer of Cherie Booth. When you learn more about her life, as I hope you will when you've read this book, you may well feel that this woman could be an excellent role model for young girls today, if only they were allowed to know more about her.

One

SOMEBODY'S DAUGHTER, SOMEBODY'S WIFE

On the day her husband was chosen to be leader of the Labour Party in July 1994 Cherie Booth said wistfully: 'I started life as the daughter of someone, now I am the wife of someone, and I'll probably end up as the mother of someone.'

Of course everybody is somebody's daughter. Cherie's problem was that she was the daughter of someone famous. Cherie spent her childhood trying to escape the publicity surrounding her famous father, the actor, Tony Booth – best known for his role as Alf Garnett's son-in-law in *Till Death Us Do Part*. At school it was the first thing other kids said about her. 'Do you know who her dad is?' Boys who fancied her as a teenager said that having a famous father added to her attractions.

When her husband Tony Blair first met her he was astonished at whose daughter she was. For the first few years of their married life, whenever her name was mentioned Cherie continued to be described as the daughter of Tony Booth. Even Tony Blair did it. When he was trying to get onto the shortlist to be the Labour candidate for Sedgefield in the 1983 General Election he promised that Tony Booth and his lover, Pat Phoenix from *Coronation Street*, would come and canvass for him. Indeed the only time the local paper showed any interest in Tony Blair was when his famous 'in-laws' appeared.

Nine months later when the Blairs' first son Euan was born, the *Darlington Echo* reminded its readers who his granddad was. Tony Booth was still the most famous person in the family.

Under a photograph of the new baby and his proud parents, the caption read: 'The 5lb 12oz baby boy born in the public ward of St Bartholomew's Hospital is the son of the Sedgefield MP Tony Blair. His wife Cherie is the daughter of actor Tony Booth who recently announced his engagement to Pat Phoenix, Elsie Tanner of *Coronation Street*.'

It was ten years later on 21 July 1994 when Tony Blair became leader of the Opposition that Cherie's role was transformed from somebody's daughter into somebody's wife. Cherie had fought desperately for Tony to win the Labour Party leadership. His main rival was Gordon Brown, and the Blairs worked together to defeat him. But Tony's victory wasn't a sign that Cherie was going to give up her own ambitions and coast along by his side. She and Tony had always been equals. They were both successful barristers, although she had done better in her law exams. They had both been parliamentary candidates in the 1983 election, and when Tony was elected and she was not, she shrugged her shoulders and pushed ahead with her legal career.

The last time Cherie ever gave an interview about her private life and her relationship with her husband was well before the 1997 General Election when she made it clear that they would continue to have an equal partnership and she would continue with her own career.

Once Alastair Campbell joined Blair's team as Chief Spokesman after the leadership election in 1994, a strategy was developed about the part Cherie would play in her husband's political life. Lord Irvine had brought up the topic soon after Blair became the Labour leader: 'What shall we do about Cherie?' he said. It was agreed that she would become the 'Silent Spouse', attending public events with her husband as much as possible but never commenting or being interviewed. The journalist Susan Crosland was commissioned to write a profile of the Blairs for an

American magazine just before the 1997 election. Tony Blair's office agreed access to 'Friends of Blair' and to top lawyers Lords Falconer and Irvine, Michael Beloff QC and Maggie Rae. Then Susan Crosland asked Alastair Campbell for an interview with Cherie. 'Never, never, absolutely never,' he replied.

This strategy has lasted to the present day. The journalist Anne McElvoy was commissioned by Tina Brown of *Talk* Magazine to write a profile of Cherie for the run-up to the 2001 General Election. McElvoy was allowed to watch Cherie giving a speech. She was treated to a few off-the-cuff comments on pregnancy from Cherie (McElvoy was pregnant at the time) and a few sharp remarks from Cherie's aide Fiona Millar. That was it. There was no interview with Cherie and an interview which McElvoy had arranged with government minister Margaret Hodge, friend and former neighbour of Cherie, was withdrawn at the last minute because Downing Street said it had been organized without permission.

Cherie's last public words on her relationship with her husband demonstrated that she had no idea how much her life would change when he became Prime Minister.

'The fact that Tony's fairly famous and I'm not doesn't bother me at all. I'm well paid and highly regarded in my own field. As a barrister, I'm a woman in a man's field and I'm certainly used to holding my own.'

Her future as an individual 'holding her own' was doomed. From now on the people who wanted her to take up their cases would be influenced by whose wife she was. Some would want to hire her because she was the wife of the Labour leader, others would reject her for the same reason. It didn't matter how clever she was or how hardworking, how imaginative or inspired, from then on the most important fact about Cherie Booth was that she was Mrs Tony Blair.

Of course this was the last thing Cherie wanted. She had hated all the publicity her father attracted when she was a child, feeling humiliated and embarrassed by it. Although she hadn't seen much of her father after he left his first family for good just after the birth of the only other child of the marriage, her sister Lyndsey, he seemed to be on the television every week and his wild goings-on were endlessly reported in the papers. Every girl in the playground and every potential boyfriend knew who her dad was, and she feared that they might judge her accordingly.

Cherie Booth realized that unless she was very careful her own children could be subjected to the same sort of misery she had suffered as a child. She made some tough rules. The children were to have as normal a life as possible behind a wall of press silence. Except for an annual photo opportunity they must be allowed to go about their daily lives unphotographed and unremarked on.

With the help of Alastair Campbell and his team, Cherie then decided how she would run her own life. In fact she would have two lives. There would be two Cheries. 'Cherie Booth' would go on being a barrister, absolutely independent of her husband's government. Like other top silks she would take on whatever suitable work was available and if that involved fighting against the government she would relish the fight. As Cherie Booth she would also be a mother and a citizen, keeping well away from the media spotlight, protecting her family and demanding the right to a private life where she could go shopping, travel on public transport and attend events at her children's schools without being under constant observation.

The role of 'Cherie Blair', on the other hand, would be just that – a role she has learned to play with increasing polish. Cherie had always loved acting and has always been good at it. As Cherie Blair she would emerge from the wings, look out over the footlights and play the part of a loving wife at her husband's side.

What was so curious about it, however, was that it was to be strictly a non-speaking role, which she first played with some success during the 1997 General Election. For six weeks she appeared every day on the campaign trail. She was at Blair's side at the count in Sedgefield, flew down to London, attended the victory party and walked in the front door of Number 10 Downing Street with her husband's arm around her shoulder, without ever speaking a word in public.

After eighteen years in the wilderness of opposition the Labour Party's foot soldiers – the backbenchers and their wives and secretaries and researchers – marched into London on 2 May 1997 expecting to be part of a great transfer of power to the people. Everyone had their own favourite scenario of how things might change. My husband, Austin Mitchell, a backbench Labour MP, thought there would probably be a symbolic gesture and the great steel gates Mrs Thatcher had installed in Downing Street would be pulled down and taken away. But nothing like that happened and four years later the gates are still firmly in place and firmly closed.

My own dream was that the new government would mark a fresh beginning for British women. The new Prime Minister's wife was a feminist, a working mother with ideas of her own who would surely make her husband listen to women's views and act on them. She would be a highly visible role model for young women everywhere. I was even hopeful that for the first time Westminster women, whether MPs, workers or wives, who had so far lived and worked in the atmosphere of a male club, would have a voice at last. In fact most women who were interested in changing and improving women's lives invested the now powerful Cherie with the hopes of us all. This book is in part an attempt to assess whether and how Cherie Blair Booth has used her undoubted influence.

My first meeting with Cherie and Tony came just a couple of weeks after the 1997 General Election when they invited us round for a drink. Members and spouses were called to a reception at Downing Street. Of course there wasn't room for Labour's enormous majority to attend all at once, so we went in regional groups. Austin is the MP for Grimsby in Lincolnshire, so most of the members of our group were from Midlands seats. There was Joe Ashton from Bassetlaw and his wife Maggie. Tony Benn from Chesterfield and his beloved Caroline. There was Robin Corbett and Val, Bruce Grocott and Sally, Helen Brinton and her then husband who was an English teacher at Dulwich College.

The first person I saw when I entered the Downing Street reception room for the first time was Cherie. She looked slim and chic in a knee-length brown print frock and was surrounded by adoring wives and shy husbands. She nodded frequently and smiled nervously, tipping her head up like a bird as she listened to what they had to say.

Tony made a short speech about how great it was going to be now we were in power. Because I thought that this was bound to be the first of many such evenings I was content to sit on a window ledge with Caroline Benn. She wondered idly if they still had rats at Number 10. 'I was last here when Tony was a minister in Harold Wilson's day,' she said. 'The place was overrun. You could see mice peeping their heads out from the skirting boards during receptions, and worse down in the basement.' Towards the end of the party I found myself briefly in the circle running round Cherie. She smiled. 'I haven't seen you in Sainsbury's yet,' I said, trying to be funny. She took it kindly and said she was still doing her shopping near where they used to live, and moved on. I cursed my stupidity and vowed to ask her something sensible the next time we were invited.

A few days later Sally Grocott, wife of the Prime Minister's Parliamentary Private Secretary Bruce, and Val Corbett, wife of Robin, the Chair of the Home Affairs Select Committee, announced that they were starting a new group called the 'Spouse in the House Club' for the partners of Labour MPs. 'Partners' was a new word at Westminster. Before the 1997 election no one could have admitted to living with someone without being married to them. Now suddenly there were MPs, ministers even, who'd been living for years with people to whom they weren't married. There were gays in the cabinet and their partners were going to be 'spouses' just like the rest of us. *The Times* revealed that Doran, partner of Chris Smith was swapping recipes with Mrs Frank Dobson.

Perhaps most significant of all these unmarried partnerships for those outside the magic circle was that of Alastair Campbell, the Prime Minister's Official Spokesman, and his girlfriend and mother of his children, Fiona Millar. Fiona, too, was given a job at Number 10, working with Cherie. Officially she worked for the Visits Department, unofficially she became Cherie's minder. Well before they all moved into Downing Street the Blairs, conventionally and happily married themselves, tried to persuade Campbell to marry Millar. Campbell and Millar resisted the persuasive efforts of the Prime Minister and Cherie and remained resolutely unmarried.

Looking back on this period, this really can be seen as the New Labour dawn, when life felt more relaxed because at last people were being open about their private lives. We all considered, misguidedly, that this relaxation of the restrictions on the way people ran their private lives would signal other big changes in the way we lived and worked at Westminster.

In tune with the new spirit temporarily alive at Westminster, several jolly letters arrived in MPs' postbags encouraging all spouses to meet for a drink on the roof terrace at Number 1 Parliament Street and follow it up with a dinner upstairs at the Albert Pub in Victoria Street. I sent off my acceptance. Then another message arrived containing a warning. News of the meeting had been leaked to the papers by people who wanted to do the Labour Party harm, and had appeared in a diary column. The party would therefore be on 'lobby terms'.

The lobby are the journalists whose job it is to report what goes on at Westminster. They are allowed to chat with Members of Parliament in the lobbies and corridors surrounding the debating chamber. When something is reported in a newspaper on 'lobby terms', the journalist retells the story without revealing who told him it. If Jack Straw told a lobby journalist that David Blunkett was about to be sacked from the cabinet, the journalist could write about it without revealing his sources. In reality this is just another Westminster wheeze for keeping ordinary people out of the loop, and it seemed hopelessly pretentious to put a restriction like that on some wifely chat over a glass of wine, but the organizers had already been upset by the newspaper diary piece.

We paid £25 a head for a glass of champagne, a roast dinner from the buffet and some red wine in a carafe. It was surprisingly good fun. Thirty or so spouses turned up, including a couple of men. I'd never really met many other members' partners before and I enjoyed hearing about their lives and discussing problems we all shared. Then came the evening's big attraction. Cherie appeared fresh from her chambers in a pinstriped trouser suit. She was followed by a bustling Fiona Millar, already firmly installed as Cherie's minder. We all sat mid-munch and Cherie walked from table to table asking us questions about who we were and where we came from. It was embarrassing to try to chat with your roast beef cooling on your plate. It felt like teatime at an old folks' home when the Mayoress arrives unexpectedly, or maybe a coach trip to Blackpool when someone important hops on the bus on the outskirts of town to wish you a happy day out. Val Corbett gave a brief speech telling us how important it was that spouses got together in the new parliament and promised that we might even get invited to take our kids on a picnic in the grounds of Dorneywood if Pauline Prescott could be persuaded.

A few days later I wrote a light-hearted piece for a newspaper about my adventures on the Spouses outing. Instantly it was made clear to me by email from Val Corbett that my behaviour was disgraceful, dishonourable and unforgivable. I'd been allowed a tiny glimpse inside the top people's tent and I'd sold my story. Just weeks into the new government I had really let the side down with my disloyalty. I was banned for life from the Parliamentary Spouses group. At the Labour Party conference some months later I said a cheery hello to Robin Corbett. He responded warmly in earshot of several other people – 'What an absolute shit you are . . .' – and proceeded to highlight what he felt were other 'attractive' aspects of my personality.

Robin Corbett's loyalty was rewarded with a peerage. I never saw Cherie in private again. But neither did anyone else.

The woman who had visited the Spouses club had been Mrs Tony Blair in her role as the Prime Minister's wife. Cherie Booth QC was to remain a strictly private person, certainly not available to fight for women's rights or act as a role model from a platform at 10 Downing Street. Her only public speeches were in sessions with lawyers or for charities she supported. Cherie Booth QC was off limits to ordinary folk, just as she had planned.

The more determined Cherie was to hide her real self away,

the more fascinated people became. Who was the silent woman at the Prime Minister's side? What was she really like? Rumours abounded. Some said she was far to the left of her husband, almost a Trot, whose vow of silence was necessary because of her extreme views. Others reported that she was much cleverer than her husband and she had to be kept quiet lest she show him up in public. There were tales that she was bossy and assertive and she was a cross between a First Lady and Lady Macbeth. Like all the best rumours there were little shreds of truth hanging on the bones of the stories. There were also some quite meaty chunks of misogyny. Denis Thatcher trundled along amiably in his private capacity and was never subject to the same kind of scrutiny that Cherie as a successful woman was going to be.

Cherie's enthusiasm for rigidly dividing her life into two spheres was encouraged by Alastair Campbell from the moment he became Blair's Press Spokesman, and he instructed his partner Fiona Millar to enforce it. Once the election was over and the Blairs were safe in Number 10, Campbell and Millar zipped up the tent flaps and excluded the world from the Blairs' private lives. The excuse was always the same: the children's privacy.

What emerges from the edifice they have constructed are snippets that distance them from the ordinary electorate; rumours of Cherie's love of the lavish seep through. The Blairs seemed to be very keen on a luxury lifestyle surrounded by celebrities. In fact the Blairs had discovered that the rich and famous were the real experts at keeping their private life private from nosy journalists. So ownership of a chateau or a luxury villa in France or Tuscany was a good start to becoming a friend of the Blairs. Holidays were taken behind castle walls in exotic foreign locations with entourages of nannies, relatives and helpers.

Cherie was criticized for her lack of style and zing when she first began to appear with Tony, so she hired a style adviser. Her clothes, which had originally come from the High Street, moved through a boutique phase to middle-class professional and on to some of Britain's best designers. Princess Diana-like, she started appearing in Shalwar Kameez on suitably ethnic occasions. The Hindujas gave her a beautiful and expensive outfit chosen by a Hinduja daughter, but Cherie, proving herself smarter than some cabinet Ministers, decided that it wasn't suitable and returned it.

She paid thousands of pounds to take her own hairdresser with her on foreign trips, and is said to have spent thousands more on her favourite accessory: shoes. There are murmurs about crystals and alternative medicine including secret visits to an elderly body dowser in Byfleet who helped her through her pregnancy with Leo.

This obsessional secrecy fuelled the reputation Tony and Cherie are gaining for being much grander than previous Prime Ministers and their families. The Majors were positively mouse-like in their modesty; Margaret Thatcher didn't really enjoy breaks away from her job, and kept celebrities firmly in their place; Harold Wilson took his holidays in the Scilly Isles. There has never been another family like the Blairs in Number 10, and there has certainly never been a leader's wife like Cherie.

And for all the publicity they get, the Blairs remain an enigma. For all his appearances and pronouncements, commentators still speculate endlessly about what Tony Blair really thinks and feels. Cherie Booth's rigorous avoidance of public scrutiny only succeeds in making us even more curious about her. We talk and write about the peripheral things – the holidays, the clothes, the celebrities they entertain – because we are not allowed to know anything about the real Cherie.

When I first became aware of Cherie it seemed to me that here for the first time was a woman who had achieved real equality with her husband and had used it to further her own career. Now that her husband had become the Prime Minister, Cherie seemed set to go on to further success herself without jeopardizing her relationship or her family. How did she manage it? What lessons could she teach the rest of us?

The story of the real Cherie is of interest to all women who see her as a role model, if not for themselves, then for their daughters. But so far that story has been denied to us. All we are allowed to see is a supportive wife standing in silence at her husband's side. Far from being a positive role model, it reinforces an outdated idea of a woman's place.

The part of Cherie Blair was upgraded to a speaking role for the 2001 General Election campaign. Occasionally she was heard to joke with sexy young men and chat warmly with mothers about their babies. Tony Blair gazed at her with admiration when she joined enthusiastically in a pensioners sing-song: 'If you were the only girl in the world', they sang heartily, and Cherie with a big smile turned to encourage her man. Tony was bashful, embarrassed and didn't know the words.

The day after that second election victory there was a family photocall on the steps of Number 10. Tony and the boys were kitted out in modern suits and wide ties by British celebrity designer and Number 10 party-goer Sir Paul Smith. Kathryn and Cherie in pale summer colours looked feminine and decorous. There was a cameo appearance by baby Leo. Then the Blairs waved goodbye, stepped back into their tent and closed the flaps.

This book is an attempt to understand better the woman inside the tent. It seems that Cherie was a star from an early age.

From the day she arrived at infant school she was spotted by staff and children alike as someone absolutely brilliant and outstanding. Small boys worshipped this princess from afar. Small girls were in awe of someone so confident who appeared to know her own worth. Her mother, Gale Booth, says Cherie has never given her a minute's worry – ever.

Can she really be such a paragon of virtue, and if she is, why doesn't she want the world to know about it?

This is the story of the perfect life of Mrs Blair.

Two

BEGINNING IN BURY

On Monday 2 April 2001 Tony Blair was due to announce the date of the General Election. Everyone at Westminster had known for at least a year that Labour wanted to go to the polls on 3 May, the same day as the local council elections. It was assumed that the Prime Minister would visit the Queen on Monday morning and make his announcement to the Commons in the afternoon. Cherie Blair was due to visit Liverpool's John Moores University, where she is Chancellor, and was booked for a quick side trip to Lancashire to lay the foundation stone for a new maternity unit where she could highlight Labour's achievements in the health service.

But the election was not announced. An epidemic of foot-and-mouth disease in British cattle and sheep and the intervention of leading churchmen on behalf of the suffering rural population put a stop to all that. The Archbishop of York pleaded publicly with the Prime Minister to delay the election and Tony Blair, always keen to be seen to be doing things the right way, acceded to the churchmen's requests. He came out of Downing Street that Monday morning and simply confirmed what the *Sun* newspaper had announced on Saturday: the local council elections would be put off until 7 June.

The maternity unit Cherie was scheduled to open would not be completed for several months but the visit went ahead. Local Members of Parliament were booked to escort her, the northern press had been primed and hospital staff had received bright yellow photocopied fliers asking them to gather in the grounds of the hospital at 2.45 p.m. for the visit of Mrs Cherie Blair, the Prime Minister's wife.

Cherie left early from lunch with the great and good at John Moores and headed for the Metropolitan Borough of Bury. She had a very special personal interest in the town she was about to visit. Bury, along with Bolton and Rochdale, is one of the old textile towns on the northern outskirts of Manchester. Each has its own proud history, its own local heroes. The world knows that Gracie Fields was a Rochdale lass. Bolton was the birthplace of Samuel Crompton, inventor of the Spinning Jenny, while Sir Robert Peel, the nineteenth-century Home Secretary who began the Metropolitan Police Force and went on to become Prime Minister, was the son of a wealthy Bury industrialist. The *Millennium Guide to Bury* devotes three pages to 'Native Sons and Daughters'. As well as Peel, the town produced the first President of Harvard University, half a dozen judges, world champions in cycling and snooker, Richmal Crompton, author of the *Just William* books, and entertainer and musician Victoria Wood. There is no mention at all in the *Guide* of arguably the most influential woman in Britain today: Cherie Booth was born in Ward 3 of Bury's Fairfield Hospital on Thursday 23 September 1954. Bury Public Library has some wooden box files containing notes and clippings about local worthies but there is nothing at all about the Booth family or Cherie. The only mention of the connection is the Birth Announcements in the *Bury Times* for Saturday 25 September 1954:

> HOWARD BOOTH On September 23rd 1954 at Fairfield General Hospital, to Gale and Tony, a daughter (Cherie). Thanks to sisters and staff of Ward 3.

Who or what was Howard? There is no mention of this name in Tony Booth's biography. Cherie's mother was called Joyce Smith when she married Tony Booth just six months earlier at Marylebone Register Office in London. Joyce's mother was Hannah Smith and her father was Jack, a coalmining overseer in Ilkeston in Derbyshire. Joyce had one brother, Stewart, four years her senior. It's not hard to guess that Gale changed her name from Joyce, because Joyce is not the most glamorous name for a young woman of twenty-one with dreams of a career on the stage – at least until baby Cherie came along. Was Joyce Smith now an actress called Gale Howard? Were the Booths just indulging in a little early feminism and announcing baby Cherie in the names of both her parents? But no one in the theatre had ever heard of Gale Howard.

None of the mothers I could find who had babies on Ward 3 could remember Gale, Tony or Cherie. Cherie's birth certificate is straightforward: Cherie Booth, daughter of Tony and Gale. When she was born, Cherie's parents were living at 198 Walmersley Road in Bury. Walmersley Road is a ribbon of Victorian mansions interspersed with clutches of local shops, 7-11s, chippies, balti houses and an unlikely feature of Bury life, sun bed centres. There are invitations to pick up a smooth golden tan on hoardings and walls all over the town.

The building at 198 Walmersley has half a dozen bell pushes at the side of the door, some sturdy greenery in the garden and a broken 'For Sale' sign lying in a strip of mud which might once have been a herbaceous border. It looks like a rooming house. In the 1950s it might have been flats or even theatrical digs. The 1954 register of electors gives Clifford and Constance Fellows and Harold and Elizabeth Holliday as the residents of 198 Walmersley Road, but electoral registers are compiled in the October of the previous year. In the 1955 register Anthony Howard-Booth, Gale Howard-Booth and Geoffrey Owen-Taylor have replaced the Fellowses and the Hollidays at 198. But still no clues as to where the Howard came from. Double-barrelled surnames were certainly unusual in the Bury area in the 1950s: I couldn't find more than a handful in twenty pages of the electoral register. Perhaps they just got the idea from their flatmate Geoffrey Owen-Taylor, who turns out to have been another actor last heard of in Australia in 1972 as the producer of a pair of TV specials starring Sid James.

Apart from the birth announcement there is little trace of the Booths or even the Howard-Booths in Bury. Bob Hargreaves, the town's historian, is keen to celebrate Bury's most famous daughter, but until her return visit on 2 April 2001 he had few facts to go on. Cherie had made a previous flying visit organized by the Bury North MP David Chaytor when she was on her way to the Labour Party Conference in Blackpool three years earlier. She'd called in to give her blessing to the first ever Bury Businesswoman of the Year awards, which were just getting under way. She hadn't been able to visit on the day of the actual presentation but she had a quick cup of tea with the finalists in a small ceremony at the town's art gallery. A journalist from the local paper had asked her about her birth in Bury but she had brushed the question aside, saying that she didn't really know too much about the details of her birth and thought her parents had just been passing through. Margaret Robinson of the Bury Hospice who was one of the organizers of the event said she knew Cherie's aunt Audrey very well, and how proud her auntie would have been of Cherie's achievements. This made it sound as if her aunt had once been living locally but Margaret Robinson was just revealing a coincidence. She'd worked with Audrey Gray, Tony Booth's sister, at the National Coal Board in Wigan many years before.

Lacking hard facts, the *Bury Times* made little of Cherie's first return visit as a celebrity. There were a couple of paragraphs and a photograph followed by three years of silence about their important daughter.

When Cherie arrived at Fairfield Hospital on 2 April 2001, she found herself with a political situation on her hands. On the front page of the *Bury Times* the previous Friday, thirteen local medical consultants had made a public apology to the people of Bury for failing them. The consultants said that ten years of underfunding to the tune of £10 million a year had led to Bury having one of the lowest numbers of doctors and nurses per number of hospital beds in the country, and they had also been tough in their criticisms of the local Members of Parliament and the government. Cherie carefully ignored the furore and concentrated for once on her personal story. She joked with the staff at the maternity unit: 'It didn't look like this when I was born.'

She told the *Manchester Evening News*: 'Most people know I come from Liverpool but in fact I was born in Bury. My parents were in repertory at the local Hippodrome Theatre, which had an organ which rose out of the floor, in a play called *White Cargo*. While my father was performing at the theatre it was announced from the stage that he had a baby girl and they played the song "Cherie I love you so, That's my desire."'(A romantic 1930s hit by Helmy Cresa and Caroll Loveday ended: 'To hear you whisper low, just when it's time to go, Cherie, I love you so. That's my desire.')

When she got back to Downing Street, Cherie told her mother about her visit to the Fairfield Hospital and Gale told Cherie more about her birth. Tony Booth had been to visit Gale in the afternoon, and they had been told that Gale would be induced the next day. After Tony had gone off to the theatre, Gale decided she didn't want to wait until the next day so she took matters into her own hands: 'I drank my cup of castor oil and there you were that night!' Gale remembered that the midwife was a very large lady indeed and that Tony had run into her on his way back to the hospital. The midwife told him the good news that his wife had given birth to a baby girl. Big as she was, Tony Booth danced her round the bus stop.

There were several puzzling errors in Cherie and Gale's version of the birth. The play performed at the Hippodrome on 23 September 1954 was called *Chinese Bungalow*, and Tony Booth wasn't included in the cast list. The organ which rose out of the floor was at the Arts Cinema, now a Bury nightclub. But a letter that appeared in the *Bury Times* on 27 April 2001 answered a lot of questions.

> Your article of 6th April regarding the visit to Fairfield Hospital by Cherie Blair and her father Tony Booth brings back happy memories of the time I worked with Tony at the old Bury Hippodrome.
>
> Tony Booth was the company's Stage Manager as well as being an actor, and I was the scenic artist for the Fortescue Repertory Company, painting a different set each week for the various types of play. I remember quite distinctly Tony and myself every Monday morning preparing the set in readiness for the afternoon's dress rehearsal prior to the evening's opening performance. Cherie Blair's mother if I remember rightly would sit in the stalls during this preparation with a critical eye for detail and knitting away at . . . what I imagined . . . were baby clothes for her future daughter.
>
> Weeks later Tony announced it from the Hippodrome stage that he had a baby daughter. Those were happy but hardworking days . . .

The letter was from Trevor Cresswell, now retired and in his seventies but still living in Bury. Trevor told me that in 1953 he started a scenery business in an old stable and used to push leaflets under the door of the Hippodrome offering to make their sets. One day he got a visit from the company stage manager Peter Adamson, who asked Trevor if would take on the painting of the scenery each week. Peter Adamson was later to become famous as Len Fairclough in *Coronation Street*. These days he's a pensioner in Lincolnshire, living quietly and spending a lot of his time reading.

'Stage management', says Adamson 'was the way into the theatre in the 1950s.' Today aspiring actors would try to get bit parts on TV but back then they would start out as assistant stage managers. They worked hard backstage and got walk-on roles as a reward. Adamson was one of the thousands of people who worked for Frank Fortescue, who lived in Birmingham but owned repertory companies all over the north. The plays were comedies, farces, mysteries and thrillers. F. H. Fortescue's Number 1 Theatre Company performed *Murder in the Shelter*, *Rookery Nook*, *She Never Had A Chance*, *My Wife's Family* and *School For Husbands* to packed houses in Bury in 1954. But television killed off the regional reps and the young people who started out in repertory in the 1950s became the first television stars.

Peter Adamson remembers Anthony Howard-Booth as a young, handsome and charming assistant stage manager who wanted to be an actor, but wanted to set the world to rights as well. 'He was a noisy political animal. Red hot, almost a Communist. I liked him very much.'

Adamson thinks he first met Tony at the Theatre Royal in Castleford, and perhaps offered him a job back in Bury – but he's not sure. What he does remember is that he didn't think Tony Booth knew much about child rearing. Peter Adamson and his wife Jean produced a baby son in June 1954 when Gale was six months pregnant with Cherie. When Michael Adamson was about a month old Tony asked Peter, 'Does he still mess his nappies?'

When Anthony Howard-Booth, assistant stage manager, announced the birth of his daughter from the Hippodrome stage after the evening performance of *Chinese Bungalow* on 24 September 1954 he was able to tell the audience that she was called Cherie.

Cherie Booth was named after the daughter of Nancy Hoyle, who ran a guesthouse in Ryader in mid-Wales. The Booths stayed with them when they were appearing at the local repertory theatre and became very fond of Nancy's little girl, then eight years old. The grown-up Cherie Hoyle now lives in Adelaide, South Australia, with her architect husband Paul Downton. Hoyle and Downton are passionate about ecology and run a project in the city centre teaching people to build their own housing out of straw bales. Cherie remembers Tony and Gale Booth well, but the two families lost touch and she didn't know what had happened to the baby girl named after her until Tony Blair was elected leader of the Labour Party in 1994 and a photograph of him with his wife appeared in the local Adelaide paper. Cherie Hoyle's first thought was that Mrs Blair looked very like her old friend Gale Booth, and then she realized that Cherie Booth QC must be Gale's daughter. 'When you are eight years old and someone tells you that they are going to name their daughter after you, it's something you take very seriously indeed. I spent a lot of time worrying about what had happened to little Cherie Booth and it was wonderful when I found out what had become of her.'

Cherie Hoyle didn't get in touch with her namesake because she didn't want it to look as if she was intruding now that the other Cherie was famous. But when she made her first visit to Britain for twenty years in July 2001 she was persuaded to write to the woman who was named after her, and as a consequence was invited to bring her family to visit Cherie and Gale at

Downing Street. In a slightly fraught meeting, made so by the suspicious Fiona Millar, who worried that it might be a press stunt, Cherie Hoyle shared happy reminiscences with Gale Booth. The Prime Minister's wife listened with interest to Cherie's own political aspirations (she intends to stand for the South Australia State Assembly as an anti-nuclear candidate): 'I got a big smile from Cherie when she heard I was standing for Parliament.' Cherie Booth mentioned that she and Tony would be visiting Australia in the autumn to attend the Commonwealth Heads of Government Conference and of course Cherie invited them to visit her Eco-centre in Adelaide. Cherie Booth said ruefully that she and Tony hardly got any free time at all when they were on official trips abroad.

Before the meeting ended Cherie Hoyle produced her camera. Naturally she was keen to have a photo of her family with Gale's family. She asked if someone would take a photograph, but Cherie Booth insisted that photographs were not allowed. This is surprising because Downing Street are usually keen to allow guests souvenir photographs of their visit. Gale and Cherie Hoyle exchanged addresses and promised to write to each other and start up their relationship again after a gap of almost half a century.

According to Nancy Hoyle, she chose the name Cherie for her daughter partly because it was unusual, for which Cherie has not always been grateful. 'I was named "Cherie" after one of my grandfather's favourite songs, "Love's last word is spoken, Cherie". I found the name a pain in the backside, especially when I was a teenager and into boys.'

Cherie Booth didn't seem entirely grateful to have been given the name either. In a speech to a theatrical charity in 1999 she told the story of little Cherie Hoyle in Wales and how the name had been chosen for her and added, 'it could have been worse. If I had been a boy my parents planned to call me after Lawrence Olivier's son Tarquin.'

Three
THE BOOTHS OF LIVERPOOL

In Britain in the 1950s the theatre attracted all the young bright stars who would today be looking for jobs in television and the media. In Bury there were three theatres which still gathered enough support to give a meagre living for hopefuls like Tony Booth. But television had begun to drain the audiences away. Regional theatre struggled on, but no job lasted long. Actors were itinerants, for plays were in repertory, seldom lasting more than a week and travelling from one town to another. Moving from one set of theatrical digs to the next was very much part of the actor's way of life.

It was an almost impossible existence for a young mum like Gale and her baby daughter Cherie. For a while Tony trailed across the north of England with his wife and baby in tow, but it didn't work. Tony was still very much a boy chasing girls. During this period he fell in love and had an affair with Pat Phoenix while they were working together at the Library Theatre in Manchester, and there were plenty of other brief romances. Matters had been made more complicated by the fact that just fifteen months after Cherie arrived Gale had told Tony that she was pregnant again with what was to be their only other child, Lyndsey Booth.

A wife and family were an impossible burden for a hopeful Romeo, and eventually Tony hit on the idea of parking his marital responsibilities with his mum Vera and dad George back in Liverpool.

Gale Booth had been Joyce Smith from a Derbyshire mining family and her father Jack worked above ground as a colliery overseer. They were a respectable non-conformist family who'd been very upset when Joyce, who had gone to London with acting ambitions, came back home in a remarkably short time to announce that she was pregnant and about to marry Tony Booth, an actor from Liverpool. Gale felt miserable and ashamed. There was no way that she could turn up again on their doorstep looking for a home for her new family, and anyway she worshipped Tony and had so far ignored his frequent dalliances. She wanted to cling on to him in whatever way she could. Living with his parents seemed the best way to guarantee the continuation of their relationship. Like many young wives before her Gale was frightened of Tony's undiminished enthusiasm for the single life and resolutely turned her head in the other direction. She didn't see what she chose not to see.

So Tony took Gale, Cherie and Lyndsey to Liverpool to stay with his parents in Crosby, and promised to visit as often as he could.

There's no shortage of Booths in Liverpool: hundreds on the electoral roll, scores in the phone book. Booths have played an important part in the city's history. The brothers, Howard, James and John were founding fathers. Langham Booth was an eighteenth-century MP, and Alfred and Charles founded powerful steamship companies. Henry Booth, a statue of whom stands outside St George's Hall, was a partner of the great engineer George Stevenson who invented the Rocket and is remembered as one of the greatest railwaymen of his generation. Many of the Booths were Irish Catholic immigrants who made a respectable living as teachers, plumbers and builders, bakers and butchers. But, like other families, the Booths had their fair share of unskilled men who worked when they could and used their ingenuity when they couldn't. Cherie's great grandfather Sidney was one of these.

Sidney Booth was a lifelong pacifist who was sent to prison during the First World War. He hated it so much he joined the army as a stretcher bearer and was gassed at Mons. Tony Booth remembers sitting in the park with him in 1939. His grandfather told him that he had a service revolver and rather than see his sons fight in another war he would shoot them both. Tony, who even at the age of eight could spot a potential drama, says he rushed home and reported his granddad's plans to his mum. Vera and all the other women in the family got together to try to get Sidney certified. They failed, but they managed to get the gun confiscated.

Tony's other grandfather was Robert Tankard, a soldier who deserted in the First World War. He ran off to Ireland, met a girl called Matilda and came back to Liverpool, his name changed to Thompson, in time to get involved with the Dockers' Union in the 1926 General Strike. He was blacked by employers and found it impossible to get work. Tony remembers that Robert used to sit outside the dock gates and cut sailors' hair as they came off duty. The sailors were short of cash for haircuts and paid Robert with whatever they had to hand. Tony says his granddad accumulated a collection of shrunken heads, African curios and trinkets which made Matilda cross. She needed money for her family, not tourist souvenirs. Robert and Matilda had two children to care for, William and Vera.

Cherie's great grandfathers on the Booth side were passionate wild men who drank heavily and relied on their wives to bring up the children, sort out the family finances and run the home. Cherie follows in a tradition of strong Liverpool Catholic women. Her grandmother Vera was a tower of strength through the years when her husband was unemployed and then an invalid. She had brought up three children and defended them all against the outside world. Later, no matter how wild the goings-on of Cherie's dad, she had always welcomed him back

26

and provided a home for him. Just as she had welcomed her daughter-in-law Gale and her tiny daughter, when Tony dumped them on her doorstep.

Vera Mary Thompson married George Henry Booth in 1931. Tony was their first son: Antony George Booth, born in October of the same year. A daughter Audrey Mary Catherine Booth arrived in 1935 and a second son Bob (Robert Sidney Booth) in 1940. Cherie's grandfather George Booth was a wonderfully talented pianist who could play absolutely anything and was a brilliant improviser. He worked on the ships down the docks as a ships' writer, recording where the ship had been and what its cargo was. But he had a terrible accident, falling into a ship's hold, from which he never fully recovered.

His son Tony Booth claims that his father's accident did a lot to inspire his socialism. George's pelvis, back and an arm and a leg were broken, so the shipping company stopped his wages and docked a day's pay for the work he missed after the accident. Vera had to take cleaning jobs to support her family. After a long period of disability, George Booth died when Cherie was about twelve years old.

George and Vera Booth were homeowners. They had been living in digs when Tony was born, but shortly after, in 1934, they scraped together a deposit on 15 Ferndale Road, a three-bedroomed, yellow-brick terraced house in a narrow street not far from the docks. This house stayed in the Booth family for over fifty years. Tony and Bob returned to it over and over again when their lives outside Liverpool took downward turns. Today Ferndale Road is crowded with the residents' parked cars, old Vauxhalls, battered Fords. Everything in this street looks hard won and much used. Over forty years ago when Tony turned up with Gale and their daughters, number 15 became a very crowded house indeed. In addition to George and Vera there was

Tony's sister Audrey, Cherie's great grandmother Matilda Thompson, and Tony and Gale themselves. Tony's brother Bob Booth spent a year or so back at home when Cherie was small. Gale Booth said years later that she couldn't remember where everyone had slept because the house was so crowded.

Ferndale Road is in a clump of streets built at the beginning of the twentieth century and named after trees. Oakdale, Ashdale, Thorndale, Birchdale and Ferndale lead from St Johns Road, a busy shopping street, to a small but pleasant park. James Robinson at number 16 Ferndale, who spent most of his life in the works department at Sefton Council, remembers his dad buying his house for him when he married in the early 1930s. He'd settled in by the time George and Vera Booth arrived a couple of years later with their toddler son Tony. Vera was pregnant with her daughter Audrey and they were joined at various times by various grandparents.

The house at 15 Ferndale Road was to remain in the Booth family until Vera Booth moved to a nursing home in Bootle just before her death in the mid-1980s. When Cherie was a child the house was pretty much the same as it is today. There's a small front room with an open fireplace, a dining kitchen and a scullery with access to a tiny square yard which lets onto an alleyway which runs between Ferndale and Oakdale. The view from the back door is the backs of other people's houses and a tiny patch of sky. Upstairs there is a main front bedroom, a smaller back bedroom and a tiny box room which looks out over Ferndale Road. When she was at Seafield Convent and working hard for her 'O' and 'A' levels, this was Cherie's room. Her mother shared the back room with Lyndsey, and Vera Booth had the big front room.

This is Cherie's only childhood home and the memories of 15 Ferndale Road are said to be very important to her. Just after the Blairs moved into Downing Street, Tony Booth boasted about staying the night there. 'I sleep in the bed my mother Vera slept in all her married life. Cherie brought it to Downing Street with her.' The house hasn't changed much today. There's double glazing and central heating and a proud couple of newlyweds as owners, but the rooms are just the same. This small house has been home to many big characters. The ebullient Tony had spent all his childhood here with his brother, sister, parents and various grandparents. In fifteen years here Cherie must have learned a lot about tolerance and sharing with others.

(Many people who have visited the Blair's Downing Street flat remark on its modesty and its homeliness. School satchels and handbags litter the hallway, a crowded family room is scattered with books and papers. Cherie is probably better than most people at adapting to the closeness of family life. A lawyer who went to talk to her there about a case says she made him a cup of instant coffee and they sat down to drink it surrounded by mountains of dishes.)

Outside her childhood front door Cherie was greeted by a crowded and busy world. It was only a few steps from 15 Ferndale to St John's Road. Today there is a butcher's and an electrical shop, two bric-a-brac and second-hand furniture shops and a generous helping of barbers, hairdressers and novelty shops. It has certainly seen better days. When Cherie came to Liverpool the street was the flourishing and busy main street of a small seaside town. Joe Riley, arts critic of the *Liverpool Echo* and in his youth a friend of Gale, says you could buy good stuff in St John's Road. There was a smart clothes shop or two and it certainly was not run down. Cherie herself points out that she lived in the only Labour part of Crosby, the rest was resolutely Conservative. Crosby saw itself then as a seaside town a cut above Liverpool and the schools and colleges in the area reflected that. John Birt, former Director General of the BBC, went to St Mary's College, only a few hundred yards from Merchant Taylors, a distinguished public school. The television presenter Anne Robinson, whose mother made a fortune selling chickens in Liverpool Market, was a pupil at Seafield Covent, where Cherie was to follow a decade later, and has said that sometimes she was driven to school in a Rolls Royce. So although Cherie's roots were resolutely poor and working class, and Liverpool Docks were only a short walk away, this was a working class area of privately owned housing where aspiration was possible. There were good schools available, and talented teachers ready to help.

St Edmund's Roman Catholic Church and school are a five-minute walk from Ferndale Road. The school opened in 1872, and the foundation stone of the church had been laid by Cardinal Manning in 1875. The school has been at the centre of the Waterloo community ever since. Tony Booth was a pupil when the Second World War began and the blitzing of Liverpool meant that a huge air raid shelter for all staff and pupils had to be built in a nearby field. An unpublished history of the school records:

> In August 1940 there were night raids on five occasions with consequent low attendances at school and on the thirtieth of August, a day raid lasting one hour five minutes gave the children their first real taste of schooling in the shelter. A quick exit from classrooms to shelter (not forgetting to take overcoats, gas masks books and pencils) had to be made in an orderly and speedy fashion, and the usefulness of constant practice was demonstrated when all were safely under cover with roll call successfully completed in two and a half minutes.

Teaching went on throughout the war and Tony Booth did well at school. He claims to have read Dostoevsky and Gibbon's *Decline and Fall of the Roman Empire* when he was only nine years old. He says he didn't know how to pronounce the names, but he loved the stories. In 1942 he passed the 11-plus at the age of ten, but had to stay on at St Edmund's with older and less clever children because he was as yet too young for the grammar school.

The war ended with the victory celebrations on 20 September 1945 and life in Liverpool slowly returned to normal. The war heroes came home and went back to their peacetime occupations or trained for new ones.

From the day that Gale and Tony arrived back in Liverpool, Cherie's father was absent most of the time. But his impact is still felt. Even today, forty years on, locals talk about Tony: 'He made the mothers at the school gates shiver with excitement,' remembered one parent now in her seventies. 'Well, he was a theatrical,' mused Miss Norah O'Shaugnessy, one of Cherie's teachers, 'so I suppose that was why he was away a lot.'

Gale told the story of his wanderings differently. 'Well, we didn't split up exactly. It was never as clear-cut as that. He met Julia and went to live with her. I was terribly upset of course – devastated, heartbroken. But that was that. I didn't sit on the doorstep or bang on the door. I thought if that was what he wanted, let him get on with it. And in the acting profession you don't look at things the same way as ordinary people.'

When Cherie went to school Gale Booth began to realize she would have to earn money to support her daughters. The feckless and much absent Tony wasn't much help in that department. Gale, who had wanted so much to be an actress, had to take a job in a fish and chip shop to support her daughters.

Sheena Needs, a school friend of Lyndsey's, now a nursing sister in Australia, recalls Gale working in the Rawson Road chippie and later moving nearer to home in a chip shop in St John's Road. 'Their mum was very friendly but I always remember her smelling of chips,' said Sheena, who went to Lyndsey's tenth birthday party in Ferndale Road. 'I remember Lyndsey being upset because her mum and dad had split up. We all knew her dad was on TV and when we were leaving to come to Oz I saw him at Lime Street Station and asked him for his autograph. He told me to get lost.'

Cherie was a sensitive and intelligent girl who must have realized early on that her theatrical parents were not at all conformist. Her cousin, Father John Thompson, son of Vera's brother William, remembered Cherie as very gifted. 'When her father moved out she took her ball back. She wasn't working and she was so clever that they put her up a year to make her work. This was with the backing of Vera, all of this. Vera took in Gale and Cherie and Lyndsey and saw them through their education, but it was Vera's house, Vera's hospitality and directness which steered them through, with the help of my parents, Bill and Alice. They were always sending me and my brother round to Vera's house to help her out in whatever way we could.'

Tony Booth walked out on his first family for good when Cherie was nine and Lyndsey was seven. It was a traumatic time for the girls and Gale seems to have coped largely by denying, at least publicly, that he had gone. Gale herself wasn't Catholic, but she was surrounded by Catholics and was a strong believer in marriage. She believed in taking her responsibilities seriously.

All this was in stark contrast to the behaviour of the man she married. By the time Tony left Gale for good he was the father of two more girls by another woman. Over the period of Cherie's childhood and young womanhood there would be three more half-sisters by two more women. Cherie knew about them but never met any of them until she was a student in London. Growing up under the shadow of showman Tony can't have been easy for the serious and studious Cherie.

Four

ST EDMUND'S
AND SEAFIELD CONVENT
SCHOOL

The Liverpool Cherie Booth grew up in was stable and supportive, if you obeyed the rules. Families stayed together (well, on the surface anyway) and it was not uncommon for people to spend their whole lives in one street or district. Everyone knew everyone else and talked about them enthusiastically behind their backs. If things went wrong in a family, or people didn't conform to the norm, the story spread like wildfire. Over everything loomed the Catholic Church, casting a long shadow of guilt on the whole community.

On 1 September 1959 fourteen five-year-olds – nine girls and five boys – arrived for their first day at St Edmund's Roman Catholic Infant School in the Liverpool district of Waterloo. All the children lived nearby. The school register looks very different from what you would expect today, over forty years on. All the new pupils had two parents living at home. Carolyn McCann, whose dad Philip and mum Julia lived at 38 Argo Road, joined Anthony Rowe, son of Anthony and Margaret of 5 Courtenay Road, and Cherie Booth, daughter of Tony and Gale of 15 Ferndale Road, on that important day. Anthony, now the proud owner of a busy restaurant at Twickenham Green near London, remembers:

> I was in the same class as Cherie Booth at St Edmund's Infant
> School. We would have been five years old. She sat on table one,

33

which was for the clever children. I sat on table seven, which was for the much less clever children. Our teacher was Miss Enright. Cherie was destined to be famous because she got the part of Mary in the Christmas Concert while I played one of the sheep. She was very pretty and I remember telling one of the other boys I wanted to marry her. I didn't impress her because my hands were covered in warts. She was definitely the teacher's pet. I was the one who got rapped on the knuckles and made to stand in the corner.

When Cherie went to school it must have been an emotional moment for her father Tony. Twenty-three years earlier his dad George and mum Vera had taken him to start his education at the same school. They'd left from the same house, walked along St John's Road and across the railway crossing to exactly the same school gate. His admission was recorded in the same register as his daughter's.

From the beginning, Cherie was a quiet and very solemn little girl. Her dad had been anything but:

> I went to St Edmund's Infant school. The boys there belonged to gangs but I didn't join one. I'd never been in a gang – I'd never been that sort of guy, and for Christ sake we were only five!
>
> Just after I'd started at the school I saw a kid I was quite friendly with being beaten up by a gang in the playground. I went to pull the lads off but they all rounded on me. 'No, no, no', they said, 'You're the one we really want', and they beat the shit out of me. To this day I don't really know why. But it taught me one thing. 'Not everyone out there loves you, Tony!'

All his life Tony Booth has been an attention seeker, claiming a role centre stage in every real life scene he was involved in from the day he started school. His daughter was the exact opposite. But this didn't mean she went unnoticed. Norah O'Shaughnessy, who at that time was teaching eight- and nine-year-olds, said that she got to hear about Cherie when she was still in the infant school. 'You know how it is. Your friends warn you about all the troublemakers coming your way, but they also tell you about the outstanding pupils. They were always saying to me, you wait till you get Cherie Booth, she's marvellous.'

Norah O'Shaughnessy lives in a neat 1970s maisonette just behind Kwik Save in the seaside town of Formby. This is where Merseysiders who've made it go to retire. And so far Norah has had a long and busy retirement. She's eighty-two. She learned to drive in her sixties, when one of her sisters died of cancer and left her a car. These days Norah is the family driver, chauffeuring around Merseyside another sister who is blind.

Norah comes from a Liverpool Catholic family of teachers. Her parents came from Ireland. She was born in Liverpool. She taught in Catholic infant and junior schools for over forty years. She did all her teaching in Liverpool, except when she and her charges were evacuated to Shropshire during the war.

After the war ended she went back to the Catholic schools around the docks in Waterloo and Crosby. It was a closed community, she said. Everyone knew what was going on inside it. Everyone knew who had problems. Who stayed. Who left. For the last thirty-seven years of her teaching career Norah taught at St Edmund's Junior school in Waterloo. Hundreds of young hopefuls passed through her hands. She saw scores of good students on their way to a successful future. Norah has no difficulty at all in naming three or four children who were outstanding in her long career.

Norah remembers Cherie clearly to this day as one of her star pupils. Cherie had a wonderful memory, she never forgot things and could understand what you were telling her straight away. She was wonderful at mathematics. She was very good at acting, but she was a very quiet girl, very unassuming. She was quiet in class, quiet in the playground and she never took the lead. She wasn't left wandering around on her own, she had her own little group of friends and was very protective of her younger sister Lyndsey, but she certainly wasn't a leader. When Miss O'Shaughnessy asked the class for a bit of oral participation, Cherie was certainly not at the forefront. She never put up her hand although of course she knew the answer. She was a very reserved girl who avoided being in the limelight and waited until she was asked individually.

When Cherie was ten she passed the 11-plus just as her father had done, won a scholarship and went off to Seafield Convent. Norah O'Shaughnessy lost touch with her star pupil but she followed her progress avidly.

Once a week Norah has her hair shampooed and set at a local hairdresser in Formby. Like hairdressers everywhere they have a selection of magazines to entertain their waiting clients. Norah was flicking through *Hello* magazine when she came across an article which featured the Prime Minister's wife and her wardrobe. 'I was absolutely amazed,' said Norah. 'All those glamorous clothes. They must have someone advising her. Cherie was never the kind of girl who was interested in fashion and what she put on her back.'

Another teacher who remembers Cherie well is Denis Smerdon, who joined the teaching staff at St Edmund's in 1956. Before he went into teaching Smerdon was a flying officer who flew 130 sorties with Belgian airmen attached to the Kent-based 349 Squadron. He strafed enemy gun emplacements in mainland Europe and escorted bombers and reconnaissance missions. He'd spent hundreds of hours wedged in a Spitfire cockpit over mainland Europe and was awarded the *Croix de Guerre* for his bravery.

By the time Cherie arrived at St Edmund's in 1959 Denis Smerdon had been nicknamed 'Biggles' by his pupils. Nora O'Shaughnessy said he used to enthral staff as well as students with tales of his Spitfire crash-landing. Denis was trapped for hours in his cockpit with the nose of his machine fast in the mud. As well as moving into St Edmund's, Denis Smerdon had become a near neighbour of the Booths. He and his wife Mollie lived with their family at 54 Ferndale Road. He was probably a familiar figure to Cherie before she started school.

Denis Smerdon was also a talented singer and choral singing was a very important part of life at St Edmund's when Cherie was there; Smerdon was choir master. The school choir entered competitions all over Liverpool and took part in an International Eisteddfod at Llangollen. In 1964 the choir recorded six songs for the BBC programme *Choir Night* and two of them were broadcast. A few years later Denis Smerdon took a couple of days off and went to London to audition for the lead role in *Fiddler on the Roof*. Topol got the part but Denis Smerdon – war ace, singer and talented teacher – was a close second.

Cherie has never lost her talent for singing. Her husband said of her thirty-five years later: 'She's got a beautiful voice and she can sing everything, anthems, boat songs, football songs.'

Denis Smerdon had one more important part to play in Cherie's life. He was the man who helped her recover when her parents' marriage broke down. When Gale Booth finally decided to stop pretending and make the split between her and Tony public in 1963, local gossip about the family had reached a crescendo – and has been continuing as background music ever since.

One woman who was at school with Cherie recalled that it was the lead story in her parent's daily gossip sessions for months. Even today people around Cherie's age talk about what a rotter her father was, and how he left Gale on her own to bring up the girls.

The adult Cherie spoke about this difficult time in her life, paying tribute to Denis Smerdon, in her contribution to a book assembled by the Dyslexia Institute, a collection of the thoughts of the great and the good about defining moments in their lives:

> I had a fairly uneventful childhood until the age of nine when my parents split up. This was fairly unusual in those days, particularly in my school which was a Catholic one. I started not paying attention to my school work. But I was lucky. I had a far-sighted school teacher who suggested to my mother that I needed a challenge and should be moved up a year in school. This proved to be a great success, and I often think I owed my later success to that teacher.

Now seventy-seven and suffering from Alzheimer's, Denis Smerdon still lives in Liverpool. His wife Mollie said: 'Denis was a magical teacher. What he did for Cherie was typical. He helped hundreds of children.' She said that their family had remained friends with Cherie and kept in touch with her: 'We are very proud of her.'

And her old primary school shares this pride. The current headmaster, Mick Birkby, is equally proud of his school, saying that even today St Edmund's offers the Catholic children of Waterloo a special start in life. He feels that it has managed to escape a lot of the educational experiments of the last thirty years of the twentieth century and still offers children with disadvantages the same chances it offered to Anthony Rowe, successful restaurant owner, and Cherie Booth QC back in the 1950s. When Tony Blair talks of his dreams of all people in Britain getting the chance to fulfil their potential because they have had a good education, he could not have a better example than his own wife's experiences as a little girl at St Edmund's.

A visitor to the school will see a warm, friendly foyer, like good schools everywhere crowded with children's art and notices for parents about school events. Amongst all this is a noticeboard with clippings about Cherie. A photograph shows the school choir in 1964 and a small sign: 'Can you recognise Mrs Cherie Blair the Prime Minister's wife?' Twenty angels all assembled and looking solemnly at the camera, with one three-quarters obscured by the child in front – Cherie, avoiding the limelight even then.

★ ★ ★

Seafield we proudly salute you,
And gladly our tribute we pay,
To joys we shall ever cherish,
When school days are passed away.

Seafield we long to be loyal,
To you and to all you proclaim,
Loyal, steadfast and upright,
And worthy of your proud name.

(Seafield school song)

Liverpool Road, Crosby, is a busy main thoroughfare. At 3.30 p.m. on a weekday afternoon it's crowded with teenagers. There are several schools within a few hundred yards: Merchant Taylors, the well-known public school, and St Mary's and Sacred Heart High School, both mixed Catholic comprehensives.

St Mary's was formerly a boys' grammar school run by the Christian Brothers. John (now Lord) Birt, ex-Director

39

General of the BBC, is a former pupil. He said in a BBC radio documentary:

> The brothers had a strong presence in Liverpool, their manifest and selfless aim the energetic promotion of a Catholic middle class. They succeeded, with a no-nonsense regime of exam-focused teaching and rote learning and I was a beneficiary. Pupils learnt in a climate of fear. The slightest shortcoming was rewarded with a stroke of the infamous strap.

Another beneficiary was Tony Booth, Cherie's dad, who passed the 11-plus and was given the same educational opportunities, though he used them differently. His time at St Mary's was as eventful as his years at St Edmund's. He hadn't been at the school long when he was back in trouble just like he had been at St Edmund's. He wrote about his effect on St Mary's in his autobiography, *Stroll On*.

> In the book room there was a ladder that was pushed along so that you could get the books on the top shelf. Dummo [Booth's nickname for the Brother in charge] was always sending me up there. One day I was standing on the ladder wearing, as always, what my mother called 'sensible shoes'. Dummo put his hand up the leg of my (short) trousers. I was so surprised that I went 'Aah-haa!' and lashed out with my foot, my heel smashing his glasses and breaking his nose.

Tony Booth says he was duly expelled for assaulting a teacher and went home and told his mother the real reason. She marched down to the school and got him reinstated after a serious conversation with the deputy headmaster.

These days the Christian Brothers have gone from St Mary's, although the school sign commemorates the fact that they were the founders of a distinguished academic tradition.

Sacred Heart Comprehensive became a mixed-sex school in 1977, but before that it was Seafield Convent school, as distinguished as St Mary's in its way and run by nuns who lived and slept on the premises. The most famous alumnae are BBC presenter Anne Robinson and Cherie Booth QC.

The school is housed in a mellow red brick building set back from the road in spacious grounds with mature trees. It looks from the outside like a small American Ivy League university. Teenagers pour out the front gates chatting animatedly in mixed groups of boys and girls. All wear the same anonymous dark clothing which could be black or navy but speaks 'school uniform'.

Inside, the building looks more like a country house hotel. There's an impressive oak central staircase and all the corridors have bands of *art nouveau* tiles in green and gold at shoulder height. Christine Donegan, an ex-pupil and now the school librarian, shows me around. 'Academically gifted girls were expected to pursue the conventional careers like teaching, medicine and the law,' says Christine, who wanted to become a Chartered Librarian and was encouraged to do so. 'I still have the greatest admiration for the nuns and the rest of the teaching staff.'

Apart from the fond memories of its ex-pupils, the distinguished buildings and the religious statues and paintings, the honours boards are all that remain of the old Seafield Convent. Mrs Donegan says no one knows what happened to the school records: perhaps the nuns took them with them when they left. Cherie Booth is commemorated on the old oak honours boards which line a long first floor corridor outside what used to be the chapel in convent days and is now the school hall. Careful gold leaf records:

1975 LL.B (1st Hons) C. Booth

Cherie, a September child but a year ahead of her peers because Denis Smerdon had promoted her at St Edmund's, arrived at Seafield Convent grammar school for girls in time for her eleventh birthday in the autumn of 1965. The strong religious figure in Cherie's life was her grandmother Vera, a devout Catholic with close relations in the priesthood who, after the troubles she'd had with Tony at the local schools, must have sighed with relief when the time came to enrol Cherie at the local Catholic grammar school. Cherie already had a reputation as a brilliant girl and a hard worker who offered the added benefits of being quiet and well behaved. Gale Booth said years later that she had never had a minute's worry with her eldest daughter.

In 1965 Liverpool was on top of the world. The Beatles were on song and Liverpool teenage culture was flowering everywhere. This was the year the Beatles wrote *Help, In My Life* and *Yesterday*. They were awarded the MBE and appeared in Shea Stadium in New York. John Lennon wrote later that 'The 1960s saw a revolution among youth, not just concentrating in small pockets and classes, but a revolution in the whole way of thinking . . . We were all on this ship in the 60s. Our generation, a ship going to discover the new world.' The newly promoted Liverpool FC, managed by the legendary Bill Shankly, were to begin their twenty year spell as one of the best football teams in the world with their first ever FA Cup win that year.

Everyone wanted to be part of the Liverpool experience and people of the right age look back on it as an important part of their own growing up. Edwina Currie, the Liverpool writer who went to Oxford and became an MP and government minister before she began her literary career, says that she often escaped from her girls' grammar school and spent her lunch hours in the Cavern Club meeting the opposite sex and not knowing what to say to them.

In the 1960s grammar school girls were being educated for a life their parents aspired to, in a world that was soon to vanish forever. For Catholic girls the situation was even more difficult. They were blackmailed into working hard and sticking to the rules in schools run by female religious zealots who were determined to produce God-fearing as well as educated young ladies. At Seafield Convent the Beatles were not a major preoccupation with the class of 1965, and boys were absolutely taboo as a subject for discussion.

Tony Blair, interviewed by the *Sun* just six months after he became Prime Minister, said that one of the great things about being in power was that you got to meet all your heroes. 'I met Paul McCartney a few weeks ago and he was a lovely guy, really down-to-earth. It was the first time I'd met him and I was thrilled, he was a total hero of mine. I did tell him that my wife Cherie used to keep his picture beside her bed. Paul said to me "Is it not there still?" and I had to tell him "No, she's got mine there now!"'

Somehow I doubted if Cherie had been so daring. If she'd possessed a photo of a pop singer, she would be unlikely to have it on display on her bedside table. The girls at Seafield, and particularly those like Cherie who were in the top stream, took themselves very seriously. The distance between Crosby and the Cavern is about three miles, but it might as well have been three hundred to the girls at Seafield where hard work, dedication and godliness were expected from all pupils. Sin and the fear of the wages of sin hung like a pall over everything.

'On Monday mornings we got down on our knees on the hard, hard floor and prayed to be forgiven for the sins we might have committed over the weekend. It's left me with dreadful hang-ups,' said Elizabeth Simpson, a friend of Cherie during her time at Seafield. 'I'm still terrified of dying and having to pay for my sins.'

Cherie and Elizabeth started at Seafield on the same day and were in the same class from the fourth form right through to the upper sixth. In their last couple of years at school they were taking nearly all the same subjects and became close friends: Elizabeth went to visit Cherie in her hall of residence in London a couple of times after Cherie became a student at the London School of Economics.

Elizabeth was a farmer's daughter who went to Seafield because that was where you went if you were a clever Catholic girl. She remembers: 'It was a convent but not all the teachers were nuns. I had a nun as a form teacher when I was in the first form, but I don't think Cherie did. There were three parallel classes. We were streamed from the second year. It was quite a big school, I think there were about 650 girls.'

The uniform was a navy blue gym slip and white blouse, navy blue and light blue striped tie, with a navy cardigan which also had a light blue stripe, and a blazer and a felt hat with a brim and an elastic under the chin. If you were caught without your hat you were in trouble. Fawn socks up to the knees in the winter, or thick wool tights completed the picture. The summer outfit when Cherie and Elizabeth started off was blue cotton with bluebells on it, with a square neck and buttoned down one side to the waist. It changed to a more ordinary gingham dress when polyester came in. You had to wear your summer dress from going back after the Easter holidays right through till September. Elizabeth can remember going back to school in April freezing to death.

Girls' grammar school uniforms were a left-over symbol of the British Empire. Wherever the map was pink, young ladies wore felt hats, gloves and suitable stockings, and paid serious penalties if they were caught without. A decade before Cherie in a similar girl's school twelve thousand miles away in New Zealand, I dressed in exactly the same outfit apart from the bluebell printed cotton. In 1970, when Cherie was in the fifth form, I stood in the sun in newly independent Harare, Zimbabwe, and watched pupils cycle out the gates of the old Salisbury Girls' High sweating in their serge gym slips and lisle stockings. Their felt hats were firmly secured by elastic for the ride home to the suburbs. On the other side of the world in Liverpool, Lancashire, it must have been tough for a working single mum like Gale Booth to spend her hard-earned cash on panama hats, felt fedoras and gabardine raincoats, but the outfit went with the education.

Elizabeth Simpson says her first day at Seafield was quite overpowering. 'The village school I had gone to was wonderful. Three great teachers, really dedicated ladies. Then suddenly you go to this school with 650 children. It was huge. But I suppose I was quite lucky because I had my older sister there and I had another sister who had just left so I was used to people going there. It must have been awful for Cherie who didn't have a big sister. In the first year we were in different classes but when you got to the second form it all depended on how well you did in your exams.' Elizabeth, careful not to tell even the smallest white lie, explains that she didn't actually sit the exam for streaming because she'd had an accident and couldn't write. She'd been put into the top stream because her elder sister was reasonably bright. Thirty years on she is still uncomfortable about it. Guilt is one of the principle legacies of schools like Seafield – perhaps the price of the excellent education.

Catherine Broadhurst was another bright girl in the 1965 intake at Seafield. She went to Manchester University and her name is next to Cherie's on the Honours Board. These days Catherine, a school teacher married to a tax inspector, has five young children and still lives in Crosby. Catherine Fleming, as she now is, is godmother to Leo Blair, perhaps marking a fresh nostalgia in Cherie for her Liverpool roots. When they were in the sixth form Cherie and Catherine were close. At lunch times they would go to Cherie's house, which was fairly near the school, and talk and sometimes do a bit of study. 'Her house was always very tidy. Grandma Booth always kept it pristinely tidy. It was a terraced house, but Cherie did have her own room. Lyndsey shared with her mum, and Grandma had the other room. So it was an all-woman household. Just once or twice I met her father's younger brother: he was quite nice and normal.'

For Cherie life at Seafield was in some ways an enjoyable challenge. For the first time she was part of a group of people who were bright and hard-working just like her. 'She didn't stand out alone', recalls Catherine. 'There were five or six of us who were pretty equal. She wasn't always top of the class.' But what continued to mark her out from the crowd was her unusual home life. Elizabeth Simpson remembers: 'She was very, very bright, but just because you are bright it doesn't mean you are outgoing. She didn't really have a normal upbringing. Back in the 1960s people just didn't get divorced. I didn't know anyone else whose parents were divorced. Probably when we were about sixteen Cherie told me that she had step-sisters. To someone like me it was a huge shock because in my family there was no one who had extra-marital affairs. Now it is so much more common. It wasn't the sort of thing you gossiped about. I probably felt quite sorry for her, but in another way I thought it must be quite nice to have a famous father.'

Everyone knew Cherie's father was Tony Booth, the actor, and many of the parents at Seafield knew Tony personally. Waterloo is a distinct district of Crosby which was then an independent seaside town on the edge of Liverpool where the Mersey meets the sea. This was the community where Tony had spent most of his life. He never really achieved a home of his own away from Ferndale Road until he married Pat Phoenix in the 1980s. Everyone had at least heard of him, and many of the fathers had been fellow pupils at St Mary's. He had a reputation as a wild and handsome charmer who had dumped his wife and kids on his mum and gone off to the bright lights boozing and (the word Tony invented himself) 'crumpeteering'.

The television sitcom which made him famous, *Till Death Us Do Part*, arrived on TV just about the same time as Cherie arrived at Seafield. Fame was almost instantaneous. Such a hit that five weeks into the first series it was beating *Coronation Street* in the ratings war, *Till Death Us Do Part* featured the Garnett family, with the main star being Warren Mitchell as Alf Garnett – famous for his scurrilous diatribes against the Labour government. Tony Booth played the part of his Liverpool son-in-law Mike. Alf and Mike fought over just about everything, including football, politics and the North versus the South. Booth's character Mike was, in Alf's words, a 'Scouse git' – a work-shy raving leftie with a chip on his shoulder. He was anti-culture and aggressively working class. When Cherie Hoyle, after whom Cherie Booth is named, saw the character on television for the first time she roared with laughter: as far as she was concerned Tony Booth was playing the part of himself. The programme was so successful that it was to keep Tony Booth on the nation's TV sets at peak time for a decade. He became a household name and was recognized everywhere. *Till Death Us Do Part* was the high point of his acting career: everything before and since paled into insignificance

Tony's home life was as chaotic as it had always been. He had now moved on to live with Susie Smith, a model and the mother of his third pair of daughters, one of whom is the journalist Lauren Booth, but the relationship was stormy. Tony came and went, drank and stopped drinking and had huge rows at work as well as at home.

Overnight Cherie's dad had gone from being a no good Scouser who'd left his family to a TV star who was playing the part of a no good Scouser on the telly.

'We all knew who her dad was. That programme was on while we were at school. We were aware of him. He was very famous, if you like that sort of thing. Shockingly so,' said Elizabeth Simpson.

The effect on poor Cherie would be hard to exaggerate. Everyone knew her father had gone away and didn't much come home to see his daughters. Everyone knew that her mother had to work hard to bring up Cherie and Lyndsey and everyone knew that the real rock in the girls' lives was Vera, Grandma Booth, who went on determinedly looking after them and keeping good home-school relations going while Gale was at work. In Waterloo everyone knew Vera Booth and praised her. She was a a very powerful woman, a star. Her strength kept the small family going through the weekly humiliation of Tony's appearances on the telly. *Till Death Us Do Part* was a big hit. Fifteen million people watched it at the height of its success. For Cherie at Seafield it must have seemed like a weekly reminder of who her dad was and what he was up to.

Knowing what Cherie had to put up with at school makes her easier to understand as an adult. There would have been whispering, jokes about what was on the telly last night. Even if the young Booths hadn't watched the programme themselves, their father's mad antics were there for everyone to see. It just wouldn't have been possible for children who went to school with the girls to dissociate the behaviour of the Scouse git on the telly from the stories about Tony Booth's treatment of his family. Cherie Booth's ferocious protection of her own children and her obsession with her own privacy becomes understandable. Just like Vera, she defends her family before everything. Her litigiousness with nannies and newspapers who dare to talk in public about the trivia of her daily life and that of her children is her version of Vera's trips down to St Mary's and St Edmund's to protect her wayward son Tony. Her experiences with her father during her childhood have made Cherie the toughest and most protective of parents.

Cherie seems to have coped with her father during her years at Seafield by steadfastly ignoring him and getting on with her own life. Elizabeth Simpson says: 'I got the feeling that Cherie hardly saw her father. She certainly didn't appear very interested in him. She didn't talk about him a lot.'

But she inherited some of his talent: Cherie was keen on acting and a very good singer. Her big chance as an actor came in the lower sixth form when they staged a production of *Murder in the Cathedral*. There's only one big role in this play and Elizabeth Simpson remembers all the girls were eager for it, but Cherie was chosen.

May Gillett, then a new young teacher, had all the right extra qualifications. She was an LRAM and a LGSM – speech and drama teaching qualifications from the Royal Academy of Music and the London Guildhall School. Miss Gillett, retired for many years, still lives in Liverpool. She remembers Cherie well, but is keen to treat all the girls equally, praising the whole class: 'They were a bright group of youngsters. It was a community effort. We all learned a great deal.'

And why was Cherie chosen for the key role of Thomas Becket? 'Instinct,' she said crisply. 'I didn't even know her father was an actor. Undoubtedly she gave an excellent performance. A very clever girl.'

The theatre correspondent of the *Crosby Herald* thought so too.

The role of Thomas Becket was admirably played by Cherie Booth whose diction was faultless and the interlude when she preached in the Cathedral on Christmas morning was delightfully restrained. Here is an actress many societies would be glad to count amongst their members.

When Vera saw how good Cherie was in *Murder in the Cathedral*, she worried that Cherie might follow 'that damn fool' (her son Tony) into the theatre.

Seafield Convent School may have given Cherie an excellent academic grounding, but it presented its students with other problems. Many pages have been written about the difficulties for girls growing up in an all-female environment, and not only was Cherie surrounded by women at school, it was the same at home. Her uncle Bob, Tony's brother, visited occasionally, and then there were her priestly cousins John and Paul Thompson, but most of the time she lived in a women's world.

Elizabeth Simpson described the situation at school as she saw it: 'Going to an all girls' school can give you hang-ups and going to a Catholic all girls' school can give you worse hang-ups! You don't have sex education, you have purity lessons. It makes my husband laugh. You do not sit on a boy's knee unless you have the thickness of two telephone directories between you and him. And you don't wear black patent shoes because they are shiny and boys could see up your dress in the reflection. You get to the point where you are frightened of boys. I was terrified. You talk about them so much, but then when you meet them you don't know what to say. You don't know how to act. There were girls in our year who did have relationships with boys from quite early on but they weren't in our class. A couple of girls in our year group got pregnant, one before the sixth form. You know: thirty years ago and going to a convent school! Shocking.

It was all hushed up. Abortions had just become legal a couple of years before but there was no question of that. They both left and had their babies.'

The girls at Seafield, like girls everywhere, did a lot of dreaming and a lot of talking about boys, and Cherie and Elizabeth were no different. When they got to the sixth form one of the ways the girls got to meet boys were in their rare joint excursions with St Mary's, the boys grammar down the road. Elizabeth Simpson remembers that one of Cherie's first boyfriends was Peter Clark, who was on the St Mary's debating team. The girls of Seafield's debating team, including Cherie and Elizabeth, attended the 1972 regional finals of the English Speaking Union competition at Llandudno. One of the boys, John Creedon, who now works for Granada Television, remembers the trip (but not that Cherie and Peter Clark were an item):

> We often used to invite the girls to our events and Llandudno was just one of a number. For us boys in a single sex school run by Irish Christian Brothers it was enormously exciting to have the girls around. Everyone fancied Cherie – but then we fancied virtually all the girls – driven mad as we were by adolescent hormones. But Cherie was exotic. She was considered the sexiest girl – it may be difficult to see now but she was very attractive and had the added interest of a TV actor father. I wasn't aware she went out with anyone from our school however.

Even then Cherie was practised at keeping her private life private.

John Creedon kept a newspaper clipping from the *Liverpool Echo* of Tuesday 14 December 1971 which records St Mary's victory in the Liverpool final which sent the boys off to Llandudno. There's a photo of the triumphant team with local bigwigs. These days John Creedon has neat short grey curly hair.

Back then it was down to his shoulders, but nothing to match Peter Clark's curly locks. Creedon said that Clark was very bright and had the hardest job on the team. He was speaker number three and had to react and respond to the other team's arguments as well as producing his own. John Creedon said modestly that his own role as first speaker was less demanding.

The *Echo* reported:

> It was a case of no words barred at Liverpool Polytechnic's John Parsons Hall last night . . . It was a test not only of vocal cords but of skill, temperament and the ability to speak convincingly and capably in public. The team that combined all that into a winning formula was St Mary's College, Crosby, whose team competed with three other Merseyside schools: West Park Grammar School, Queen Mary High School and Seafield Grammar School. Last night's topics included 'The Decline of Politics'. . .

Seafield came last. This is possibly the only recorded incident of Cherie Booth coming last in anything.

One other activity in which both sexes shared was religious study. Cherie and Elizabeth joined the YCS, the Young Christian Students. The YCS was run by St Mary's College and was one of the few joint activities between the two schools. Elizabeth remembers that their main aim in joining had been to meet boys and talk to them. Neither Elizabeth nor Cherie had brothers, so getting to meet boys, talking about them and dreaming of them afterwards was very important to both girls. But Cherie had another reason. Even though she didn't talk to Elizabeth about it much, she was a seriously religious girl who had been greatly influenced by the nuns and her grandmother and wanted to play an active part in the Catholic church.

YCS was an offshoot of Young Christian Workers which was started in Belgium to follow the teachings of Bishop Joseph

Cardijn. In the 1920s he had begun support groups for young women needleworkers and for working boys. In 1924 they banded together as a sort of religious trade union and became Young Christian Workers with Cardijn as their chaplain. The organization flourished and is still very active today. The central idea was that culture was a reflection of the taste of the masses. The modern world could not reflect the glory of the creator if the masses were alienated from culture and society. Alienation could only be cured by faith and the way to spread faith was to evangelize. If you wanted to evangelize miners or students the best people to do that were other miners and students. Student believers had a duty to spread the word to other students.

The YCS in Crosby in 1970 discussed all this very earnestly indeed, says Father Gerry Proctor, who was the leader of the student group at St Mary's School and is now the priest at St Margaret Mary's at Huyton. Proctor, a couple of years older than Cherie, became her friend when she joined the group and has remained close to her ever since. They have corresponded most of their lives and he sees her every time she is in Liverpool. Father Gerry Proctor thinks Cherie always took religion very seriously indeed, even if she didn't discuss it with all her mates. According to him, after the Second Vatican Council in 1965 which changed and reformed some church practices, there was much for students to do and discuss and Cherie was very much part of that discussion as a student in Liverpool. The church had been opened up for more community projects and for dialogue with other Christian churches. 'It was our first taste of social action based on the gospel. We discussed the role students should play in society. The YCS had a powerful effect on all of us.' The YCS was schools-based, so when Cherie and Gerry left school they moved on. He went to a seminary to train to be a priest. Cherie's choices then would have been equally well ordained.

Careers advice in girls' schools can be rudimentary. At Seafield, teaching and some form of medicine – usually nursing – were advocated as the main routes for girls who had done well in the sixth form; anything else was exotic and outside the experience of the nuns and the staff. Girls whose fathers were in business or accountancy or other professions with which the nuns weren't familiar sometimes managed to follow in their father's footsteps, but not often. Cherie Booth's decision to study law may well in some part have been based on what she was learning in the YCS. Bishop Cardijn's theories had a practical base. He had started trade unions for workers, and turned them into believers. The treatment those workers got from their employers, and how it could be improved, was an important part of Cardijn's evangelizing Christianity. It was also highly political and may well have influenced Cherie.

Thirty years later at a Downing Street reception for children, a teenage girl asked the Prime Minister's wife what had inspired her to take up law. 'At the time I didn't know whether anyone inspired me, really. I just took arts "A" levels and I knew that I didn't want to be a teacher, which is what the nuns encouraged the girls to do because it's a very good thing for a good Catholic mother to do. We used to pray for vocations with our fingers crossed! But I had a boyfriend at the time and his mother said to me "You're very good at debating: why don't you try the law?".'

This was almost certainly Mrs Clark, mother of Peter, a key member of the St Marys' debating team and also a member of the YCS. Peter himself went on to do a Bachelor of Science degree in Physics at Sussex University. Cherie took Mrs Clark's advice seriously, but she was also influenced by her grandmother Vera.

Cherie says Vera was so fascinated with the law that sometimes she would go down to the law courts on Liverpool to listen to the speeches: 'There was a very famous Liverpool woman called Rose Heilbron QC, the first woman QC. She was very well known in Liverpool and my grandma used to occasionally go and see her in court. So maybe, thinking back about it after all, it had an influence on me as well. I thought that if Rose Heilbron could do it then maybe I could too.'

In 1972, Cherie got four A grades in her 'A' levels and a County Major Scholarship. These no longer exist, but were designed to enable clever young people from poor families, like Cherie, to attend university. These days someone in the same position as Cherie would need to take a loan. They would still end up with a degree but thousands of pounds in debt. Cherie went off to the London School of Economics, which had earned a reputation in the 1960s as the home of left wing radicalism. Life was much quieter now, but it's easy to see why the young Cherie Booth would have been attracted to the LSE.

Five

LONDON LAW

Cherie arrived at the London School of Economics at a quiet period in its history, but its reputation for left-wing politics had probably encouraged her to choose it over the more middle-class options of Oxford and Cambridge. In the late 1960s young people around the world had demonstrated on the streets and occupied colleges and universities. Everywhere students protested about the Vietnam War and took up the mantras of the far left. This turmoil was mirrored at the LSE and many there took part in the Grosvenor Square rally of 1968.

But by the time Cherie arrived in the autumn of 1972 things had quietened down considerably and politics had returned to classroom discussions and student societies. This suited Cherie, who was a natural swot and certainly not a trouble-maker or protester, unlike her father Tony, a firebrand Socialist. Apart from her father, who caused family rows at election time when he put his Labour posters in Vera's windows, Cherie came from a traditionally conservative house-hold. Her involvement in YCS might have moved her leftwards politically – in fact she joined the Labour Party at the age of sixteen – but by the time she got to the LSE her activism had lapsed. She claims: 'I wasn't very active in the party while I was at the LSE. I wasn't particularly interested in the Students Union and used to go home to Liverpool a lot, where I still had a close circle of friends.'

Cherie had been a much admired figure back home. The nuns, her teachers and her schoolmates had acknowledged her brilliance. In her family she was seen as a good girl. Boys admired her as a distant princess, dark, intense and self-contained. After all this admiration and hero worship, Cherie found herself on her own in a world where her intelligence alone was no longer enough to bring gasps of admiration. Universities were full of bright brains. Most students brought other attributes and interests with them.

Cherie had terrific powers of concentration and an ability to give herself totally to the project in hand. She did this so successfully and worked so hard that she went almost unnoticed at the LSE. Many of her contemporaries could not remember her. One said that he knew her quite well now and met her socially, but never realized that in a previous life she'd been in his class. Professor William Cornish, who was a Head of Department, admired her quiet intelligence. No one at all remembered her as exciting or stimulating or fun to be with. Perhaps she saved that side of herself for her home town.

Christopher Peace was an exact contemporary of Cherie's at LSE. He was in the same class and took the same law degree, but he came from a very different background. He'd been privately educated at Silcoates School in Wakefield, Yorkshire, a top northern independent school which was begun in the early nineteenth century to educate the sons of non-conformist ministers. When Peace went there it had become an expensive private school for boys from middle-class families.

Today Peace runs his own law firm in Sheffield, mainly engaging in legal aid work. Peace deals with the criminal side of the business. He has a couple of partners who are specialists in family and employment law and all the other matters which cause ordinary folks to call a solicitor.

Peace went to the LSE because he was busting to get to London: 'I thought it sounded like a laugh. Being in London would be fun, and it was! On any given day Reggie Maudling or Vanessa Redgrave would turn up to talk to the students. I remember Michael Heseltine coming, and Michael Foot. Tony Benn came to give us lectures about the constitution. It was a wonderfully lively, exciting place to be but I was naïve and a bit immature, I suppose. I couldn't believe how boring the law turned out to be. Such boring stuff to plough through. It was like being locked in a sensory deprivation tank. Frankly it was desperately dull. I thought, a bit like old Magnus Magnusson on *Mastermind*, "I've started so I'll finish"! Within a term all intellectual stimuli had ended, so I just concentrated on having a great time. I was into drama and opera and I went to the pub a lot.'

Peace looks back on his student days with pleasure. He loved the political atmosphere of the LSE, with famous people coming in to talk to the students. He loved all the extracurricular activities that students could join in, and he loved the excitement of London. He can recall very little about his eighteen or so classmates, except for the three who were female. Caroline Grace was very pretty, and then there was Jeanettte Szostak and Cherie Booth.

'Cherie', says Chris, 'was a mild source of interest because she had a famous father. She had a fringe and long hair and was quiet and very intense. She was incredibly hard working. We'd all go off for a pint and come back and she'd still be there, working away.

'I remember once we went on a trip to Wormwood Scrubs to see what the inside of a prison looked like and of course the men there were very interested in the girls in the group. Caroline Grace attracted a lot of attention because she was so good looking. Cherie? Well, she's an awful lot prettier now than she was then. I'm afraid I thought she was prim and strait-laced but then I was putting pretty nearly all of my efforts into having a good time.'

Chris Peace and Cherie Booth came from opposing backgrounds. He was a middle-class public school boy. She was a poor working class girl from Liverpool who got to university on her brains alone, while above all else Christopher Peace wanted to have a good time at university. Cherie believed that for her hard work was the only way forward and left with a first in her LL B degree. Chris left with a third. Today he is a hard-working solicitor in a northern industrial city getting his satisfaction out of representing the poor and inarticulate – doing his bit, he hopes, to iron out the inequalities in society. He's a long way from Downing Street.

Neal Stone was also in Cherie's class at LSE. Like the great majority of his colleagues he was awarded second class honours in his LL B. final examination. He also remembers Cherie Booth, but his recollections are more favourable than Chris Peace's.

'Cherie Booth was memorable in terms of her brightness and sociability and the fact that she was a student who you studied with who was good company, was helpful, encouraging and obviously, had, a very, very bright future. I mean she stuck out. There's no doubt about that. People talk about their aspiration of getting a "Good Degree". She said quite openly to her fellow students that her aim and her aspiration was to get a First, and she made that clear before the exams. It came over in a confident way. It wasn't arrogant, it was based on the fact that she worked incredibly hard. But she was also intellectually very, very bright. So that came over as an aspiration which was realistic and achievable, and she put over in a way that did nothing to undermine anyone else's confidence. She had a vision of her future and expressed it. She shared that vision with others. I remember a discussion – it may have been before the Easter break in Final Year when people were starting to get ready, preparing for exams, and were talking about what they were aiming to do after they graduated. My recollection is that she was trying to choose between going on to do a Bachelor of Common Law at Oxford or doing her Bar Finals. She did Bar finals in the end. Bachelor of Common Law at Oxford is a post-graduate degree, which is only open to the brightest and most gifted law graduates and to think in terms of doing that, you've really got to be very, very able and bright. So obviously she'd made her mind up in terms of where her career was going and I'm speculating that she must have made a decision that it was better to get on with her Bar Finals sooner rather than later and discounted the Oxford option.'

Neal Stone said that LSE at the time was a great place for law students who were interested in politics and how the Labour Government worked. He and Cherie in their final year studied labour law and legislation.

'Labour law really provided a wonderful insight for people studying law who were interested in politics. There were some academic lawyers at the LSE who had wonderful reputations, who were wonderful to study under, like Bill Wedderburn, John Griffiths and Cyril Grumfeld. They were well connected with the Labour government. They knew ministers and were advising ministers on repeal of trade union law that had been enacted by the previous Conservative government. They gave you an insight into the workings of government that you wouldn't have got elsewhere. I think that engendered interest in politics and Labour law amongst a number of students, which might not have otherwise have happened. Those were heady times for their students like us. Lecturers and tutors were sometimes late for class because they'd rushed from a meeting with the Minister where they'd been offering advice and it was exciting to us.'

Sixty-one students completed their LL B degrees at LSE in 1976. Twenty-five of them were women. Only four people got firsts: Martin Loughlin, Jeanette Szostak, Christopher Whomersley and Cherie Booth. Cherie's was the highest first awarded. Once again by sheer hard work and diligence she got to the top of the tree and won another scholarship to spend the next year taking her Bar examinations.

Cherie started the one-year course to pass her Bar exams and began to think about the future. So far sheer brilliance had been enough to see her through and she hoped it would continue. Now she had to find someone to take her on as a pupil when she had finished her exams. Pupils were not paid, but the Inns of Court awarded scholarships so that they could get practice and learn from barristers working for established chambers.

What follows is an almost apocryphal story. In the spring of 1976 Cherie Booth turned up at the Inns of Court for an interview for a scholarship to see her though the next year. The candidates sat in alphabetical order, and next to Cherie was Anthony Charles Lynton Blair. It seems she didn't take much notice of him. Cherie of course came top in the Bar exam and was awarded a scholarship from Lincoln's Inn. In those days barristers individually chose pupils and there was probably a bit of a competition to take on Cherie, who already had a reputation for coming top in any exam she took. She was offered a pupillage at 2 Crown Office Row, chambers headed by Michael Sherrard. The man who took her on as his pupil was Alexander Irvine – now the Lord Chancellor, Derry Irvine QC.

In the twenty-five years which have elapsed since then Cherie Booth has been transformed from a quiet intense student who fun-loving Chris Pearce thought wasn't much fun to be with, into a glamorous high-flyer who was chosen by the *Sunday Times* in 2000 as the most powerful woman in Britain. How did Cherie learn that intelligence alone was not enough, and who taught her?

Six
WHEN TONY MET CHERIE

He was a middle-class, public school educated Oxford graduate. He'd taken a break after Oxford, working with a friend trying to make a career out of rock music. He had long hair, full lips and a Mick Jagger swagger. But he was also religious and idealistic. He'd been confirmed when he was at Oxford and he was thinking how politics might be used to promote his vision of a better world – a vision derived from religion but promoted by politics.

She was a deeply serious Catholic girl from Liverpool who had no money, had joined the Labour Party at sixteen, and knew that everything you get in this world has to be earned through hard work. She was dismissive of white middle-class males: she thought they'd had it easy. She wanted to become a barrister to put the world to rights, to defend people in the same way as she'd watched over her sister Lyndsey in the playground when their father's drunken womanizing had been all over the papers. She had her grandmother Vera Booth as a role model. Vera had spent her life caring for people. She fought for justice and spoke out for those she felt had been wronged, including, when she believed right was on his side, her troublesome son Tony.

Tony Blair and Cherie Booth had been students together. They had both been accepted for the one year course to become barristers. At the end of the year they had to pass an exam before they could be taken on as pupils by barristers who were already practising. The results of the Bar exam were not surprising to followers of the Cherie Booth story. Cherie came top of the Bar exams for the whole country, and Tony, who had by his own admission much more of a social life and took everything less seriously, languished somewhere towards the bottom of the middle. He'd even got some help from Cherie when they were revising.

Before they even sat the exams Cherie had been snapped up as a pupil by Alexander Irvine. Tony was left to look around for a pupillage after his results came out. He too went to see Irvine, who was so impressed with Blair's wit and charm that he decided to take him on as well. Cherie was not best pleased.

Cherie had been the obvious academic choice. She'd been consistently top in every exam she'd sat since she started at the LSE. She was the academic star of her year with the highest first class law degree the London School of Economics had awarded for years. Who wouldn't have snapped her up? Her capacity for hard work alone must have endeared her to most talent spotting chambers.

Tony Blair brought with him an average degree, a middle-class background and charm by the bucketload. In a way he was what Derry Irvine, from a working class background himself, had never been. Irvine was captivated and did something unusual. He took on a second pupil. It was assumed that this meant that at the end of the year only one of them would stay on. Cherie certainly thought that. She said in an interview with the CBS *Sixty Minutes* programme in the USA in February 1997 that Blair's arrival in Chambers 'didn't please me at all because I had been assured I would be the only one.'

What it meant was that these two young lawyers, both members of the Labour Party and both determined to get on and be the chosen one at the end of their year's pupillage, were in serious competition.

Another thing they had in common was a tendency to look at politics through a religious prism. Like Cherie in the Young

Christian Students, Blair's early involvement in politics had its roots in a Christian view of the world. Anthony Phillips who was the chaplain at Tony's Oxford college, St John's and who later married Tony and Cherie, could remember Tony clearly from his college days because he went to chapel every Sunday, not something many students did in the early 1970s. Blair was confirmed in the Church of England while he was at Oxford. The Bishop of Carlisle, Graham Dow, who was resident chaplain at St John's before Phillips, prepared him for confirmation. Charles Falconer, who knew Blair before and after Oxford, thought that he'd undergone a transformation: 'During Oxford and immediately after he genuinely became utterly immersed in a sort of Christian spiritual approach for the solution of social problems. As a Christian how do I respond to suffering, poverty, in my society – England, which featured unfairness of a deep-seated sort, more in the 1970s than now, but still very real? He concluded that the only way forward is by political action within the confines of conventional politics. Only through conventional politics can certain specific goals be obtained.'

Everyone who knew Tony Blair in the 1970s thought him charming. He wanted to be liked. He enjoyed seducing people into liking him. He found himself attracted to Cherie – 'I thought and still think she was one of the most unusual and interesting people I've met' – and set out to charm her too: 'I was attracted to her because of her looks of course, but also because she was so different. She's a one-off, unusual and totally her own person.' He thought she had an edge, a Liverpool chippiness. He might well have added that she didn't fancy him much and he wanted to change this: 'She wasn't wild about me to begin with, but I was very set on her and eventually won her round.'

It's easy to see why Cherie might have dismissed Tony. He was middle-class and easygoing. For her so far everything she had achieved was as a reward for hard work. She knew she was very clever. She was cleverer than he was academically, there was no doubt about that, but so far she was not doing as well as him in their chosen profession.

At Christmas 1975 Cherie invited Tony to a party given by a legal friend. They played a team game passing a balloon between their knees and there was physical contact. 'You get out of your work clothes and you see each other completely differently,' said Tony: 'I found her immensely physically attractive but I wanted her as a friend as well.'

Cherie had attracted men from the beginning. Anthony Rowe at primary school and John Creedon as a teenager both mentioned before anything else how drawn they were to Cherie. Both also saw her as distant and out of their league. Tony Blair said: 'The breakthrough in the relationship came when Derry Irvine, our boss, took us out to lunch to celebrate the end of a big case. The restaurant was called Luigi's – I can still remember it – and it was the longest lunch I have ever had. Cherie and I were still there in the evening and ended up having dinner too. Derry tactfully made his excuses in the middle of the afternoon but I can't really say that I noticed him going.'

But Cherie still had her doubts. 'She wasn't quite sure whether I was what she was looking for. She felt I'd had it easy which in a way I hadn't,' said Blair, completely failing to understand the natural hostility of the working-class Liverpool girl to the attractive middle-class lawyer.

Cherie's mother Gale seemed not to share her daughter's reservations. In the only interview she ever gave about her family (to David Jones of the *Daily Mail* in 1996) she said nervously when asked about the man who was now her son-in-law: 'I like Tony, he's a lovely son-in-law. I love him. I get on well with him. He's just like a son to me. I don't see him as a politician at all.'

Despite their different backgrounds, friends and family could see their growing relationship. When Cherie met Tony's father Leo after she had officially become his girlfriend and he took her to meet him, he immediately spotted her potential and encouraged his son.

Tony Blair could hardly believe the girl he was in love with was the daughter of the actor Tony Booth. Blair thought Booth looked too young to be Cherie's father, and they didn't seem to have much in common. Cherie was hard-working and serious. Her father's behaviour was just the opposite. For over a decade now he had been well known across Britain and his wild drinking and womanizing had earned him a headline or two for his chaotic private life. Since he'd walked out on Cherie's mum Gale he had produced four more daughters by two different women. He didn't marry them. He was still married to Gale, who refused to divorce him.

Tony Booth had been a socialist since he was a lad. He said he was inspired by his dad's accident down the docks and the rotten treatment he got from his employers. James Robinson who still lives in Ferndale Road remembers Tony and his mum Vera rowing at election times. Vera like the rest of the Thompsons was Conservative, and Tony caused trouble by putting Labour posters in the windows.

The writer Johnny Speight met Tony Booth at Wembley, where they were attending a Labour Party rally for the 1964 General Election. Tony Booth seemed to be present on the platform in his role of Chief Troublemaker. When George Brown announced that his brother Ron had been selected for a safe seat, Booth shouted 'Nepotism!' His colleagues on the platform tried to shut him up, but he went on shouting till some of the audience joined in.

Speight, no doubt inspired by Booth's wild behaviour, told

him about a script he'd written for the BBC's Comedy Playhouse. It was about an East End family. A bigoted father, his long suffering wife, their daughter and her left-wing husband were to be the stars. Speight had written the son's part with Michael Caine in mind, but with the success of *Alfie*, Caine had become too big a star to want the job. Speight suggested that Booth would be just right for the part. Booth agreed but came up with some ideas of his own. The son-in-law could come from Liverpool, just like him. 'Why does every witty working-class bloke have to be a Cockney? If you want me to play it why can't I be a Scouse?' Then he suggested some north–south conflict. 'He can support West Ham and I can support Liverpool.'

Speight adopted Booth's ideas and when the series began a year later, Warren Mitchell played Alf Garnett, Dandy Nicholls was his wife and Una Stubbs the daughter and wife of the troublemaker from 'Oop North', soon to be known as the 'Scouse Git', Tony Booth.

Till Death Us Do Part was an immediate hit and won an early TV ratings war when the BBC put it on at the same time as *Coronation Street*. Every year or so for the next decade there would be a new series, and the show would be as popular as ever, shooting to the top of the ratings as soon as it appeared. Tony Booth on the other hand limped from series to series, never quite getting to grips with reality. He was drinking too much, spending too much, loving and leaving his women and camping out in other people's flats and garden sheds. No wonder Tony Blair was so surprised when he discovered the flamboyant personality was the father of a very bright and serious young lawyer.

Cherie Booth remembers how impressed and proud she was as a child when her father, on one of his infrequent visits, told her he had been invited to visit Harold Wilson at 10 Downing

Street. She says it encouraged her interest in politics. In his autobiography *Stroll On* Booth describes his first visit to Number 10. He was drunk, very late arriving, and a bit of an embarrassment to everyone else present. He asked Wilson why he'd sold out on socialism, and Wilson replied: 'Not tonight Tony, this is a party, no time for politics.' But Tony blundered on about socialism. and Wilson said, 'Your trouble is Tony, you take things far too seriously.' Booth rolled off for a chat with Mary Wilson and claims to have shouted at the Prime Minister of Luxembourg, who hovered on the edge of their conversation wearing evening clothes. 'Instead of just standing there, why don't you go over to the bar and fill up our glasses?' The Luxembourger did so dutifully, and Tony, who says he thought he was a waiter, took a step back and crashed into Harry Secombe, who hissed: 'For God's sake, boy, don't make a show of the profession in Number 10.' The drunken Booth, who was belligerent to boot, shouted 'It's our house! It belongs to the people, doesn't it?' – views he probably doesn't air these days with the present occupants, his daughter and son-in-law.

When Tony and Cherie were going out together Tony Booth was still living with Susie Smith, mother of his fifth and sixth daughters, Lauren and Emma. Lauren told me that she remembered Cherie in her hippie kit, bangles and beads, occasionally babysitting her and her sister with her boyfriend Tony Blair.

When *Till Death* finished its final run in 1975 Tony Booth, out of work again, started writing a novel about espionage. He was drinking in a West End pub and of course he told the landlord that he was now a novelist, but he needed to know a bit more about spies and the like. The landlord said he had a few blokes from the SAS who drank in his pub. They'd just gone off to the Palace to pick up some medals, but they'd be back in the evening. He told Tony to come back and have a drink with them.

Of course the 'SAS' had sunk a few before they met up with their eager student and they spun him terrifying yarns about assassination squads in Northern Ireland. Shivering with fear, Tony asked them to come home with him so he could tape record their stories. Armed with a fresh bottle of Scotch, the merry gang set out for Hampstead, where Tony was living with Susie Smith and her girls.

When they got there they found that Susie, fed up with Tony's antics, had locked him out. It had happened before so Tony knew what to do. The flat was on the top floor of a three-storey block. A trapdoor on the landing led to the loft. In a cupboard by the front door there were five drums of paraffin for heating. It was Tony's habit to pile up the drums, climb up to the loft and make his way carefully along the rafters to another trapdoor in the ceiling of the flat.

The SAS men had a better idea. They grabbed some rags from the cupboard and tore them into strips and soaked the strips in paraffin. They told Tony this was the sort of thing they did all the time in Ireland. They would stuff the rags round the door jamb and light them, there would be a hell of a big bang and Susie and her girls would wake up terrified and come running out of the flat.

Tony says he told them they couldn't possibly do such a dangerous thing with his girlfriend and her kids in the flat. Hang on in there. He'd be right back. Just as Tony was making his way carefully along the rafters in the roof space there was a huge explosion, flames shot upwards, Tony lost his balance and crash-landed on a can of paraffin which immediately exploded.

Clothes and body on fire, he grabbed a fire extinguisher off the wall and crashed it to the floor. It wouldn't work. Burning like a torch Tony Booth wrapped himself in a coat, rolled over and over and down the stairs. He lost consciousness.

It took Tony Booth over a year in hospital to recover from his injuries. Nearly half his body was burned. He was in terrible pain, but worst of all he was abandoned by most of the people he had been close to. His mother and sister came down to see him occasionally, but the woman he was living with stopped visiting him and moved another man into her flat. His ex-lovers had had enough of his behaviour and tried to forget him. Father John Thompson, Tony's cousin who realized that this was the lowest and loneliest moment so far in the life of his wild and wayward cousin, made the journey south to Rickmansworth attired in all his clerical gear. He identified himself to the hospital as one of Tony's closest relatives and he was allowed to see him. Tony and John prayed together. Tony has told John since that this was the moment he started to get better.

It was soon after this that Tony's eldest daughter Cherie also started to get to know him. Cherie began to visit him in hospital every week, making the long journey to the burns hospital in Rickmansworth on the northern outskirts of London by public transport. It was 1979, the year before she married Tony Blair.

Tony Booth spent over twelve months in various institutions and in great pain as medical staff tried to grow a new outer layer of skin over his body. Sometimes it didn't work. His back had to be scrubbed raw because the gauze bandages had stuck to him. He felt his feet were about as much use as a pair of full shopping bags. Occasionally they burst open spilling their contents.

The most difficult thing Tony had to face up to was that no one seemed to want him any more. The days when women squabbled over him had finished. His eldest daughter was full of care and concern but she was sharing a small flat in St John's Wood with another girl, and she was seriously romantically involved with her fiancé Tony Blair.

Where was he to go when he got out of hospital? There was only one place – the little house in Crosby that had served all the Booths so well over fifty years. Tony went home to live with his mum Vera at 15 Ferndale Road. Once again he was broke and had to start from scratch. He had few possesions, no money just six daughters, an ex-wife and a string of ex-lovers who now had new lives and lovers of their own. At one very low point Booth called a priest to Rickmansworth and suggested that the only solution for him was to join a closed holy order. I asked Father John if it was him. 'Certainly not' he said: 'I never heard of such a thing.' The unknown priest also found the idea incredible and laughed in Tony's face. 'Impossible. Ridiculous.' Tony indulged in self pity. Even the church didn't want him.

His sister Audrey, who was by this time married to a bank manager with a young family of her own to care for in Wigan, made the journey down south to pick Tony up and take him back home. Audrey warned him that Vera was now showing signs of her age (she was 76) and getting a bit senile. But Audrey also mentioned that the problem might be caused by Vera's medication. Like thousands of other patients of busy GPs in the 1970s, Vera was on valium. Given as an aid to sleep and a relaxant, it often had serious consequences especially in the old who became dazed, confused and anxious between doses. Like many others Vera had developed the habit of taking more and more valium each day because she felt so anxious and down between doses. Tony was horrified when he saw her again. His tough, alert and determined mother had changed completely. She shuffled round the house, she kept forgetting things. She spent most of her days sitting in front of the television. Tony the dreamer had believed that when he got home to his mother's house she would be at the door wrapped in an apron ready to serve him three-course meals. Instead she was sitting in a chair in front of the TV asking him what there was for dinner. Tony realized that this time there was no one to look after him but himself. Vera, after a lifetime of sorting out all the family's problems, needed help herself.

Tony was getting £17 dole a week and using it to bet on horses in an attempt to increase his liquidity. He says in his autobiography that he spent his days betting, trying to wean Vera off valium and writing a novel in the front room of 15 Ferndale. He found this very difficult. The room had never been used except for great family occasions – this was where his grandfather Robert Tankard Thompson had been laid out in an open coffin. During the whole of Cherie's childhood it was only used on very special occasions. It worried Vera that Tony was sitting in there. She would come to the door every five minutes. What was he doing? Why was there a noise? Tony felt trapped. One night sitting with Vera in front of the box he saw Pat Phoenix on *Coronation Street*. Pat Phoenix had been Pat Dean when she and Tony had worked together at the Library Theatre in Manchester when Cherie was just a baby and Tony was still supposed to be living at Ferndale Road with Gale. Pat and Tony fell in love and had an affair which ended in the way most of Tony's relationships ended: he walked out on her. They'd met a couple of times since when Tony had had walk-on parts in *Coronation Street*. She had seemed friendly enough then. Tony was lonely and broke. He decided to risk it. He called Pat Phoenix at the Granada studios in Manchester. In those days Granada was a very democratic place. The bosses Denis Forman and David Plowright sat in their offices with the doors open and without guards to keep the staff away. The cast of *Coronation Street* mingled freely with the staff of every other programme in the building. Lunch in the Granada canteen could be a fairly spectacular affair. *Coronation Street* stars and the actors in other famous programmes of the time like *Jewel in the Crown* and *Brideshead Revisited* queued up for their fish and chips (it was always fish on a Friday) or their roast beef and Yorkshire pudding just like everyone else. Quite often they would be in full costume.

Tony rang Granada and got put through to the *Coronation Street* Green Room and Pat answered the phone. She was delighted to hear from him again and invited him over to see her. They agreed to meet at the Film Exchange, Manchester's first wine bar just up the road from the studios. In the 1970s Granada had a strict 'no alcohol on the premises' policy. Tony says he had saved thirty quid from the dole and a bit of judicious backing of the horses. He set out from Liverpool to try again. A new life without booze but with Pat

The meeting was a hit. Booth and Phoenix were both feeling sorry for themselves. Phoenix had been married to actor Alan Browning who died of his addiction to alcohol. She felt she had had a dreadful time at home and at work. She was in her late fifties and she was the big star of *Coronation Street*, she was worried that the magic would fade and they wouldn't want her any more as she approached her sixtieth birthday. So both had their problems and both were delighted to find a sounding board and sympathy. Tony started spending the weekends with Pat at her home and she started nursing him. Booth's injuries from the fire were still so terrible that he had to have someone help him into and out of the bath. So far only the nurses in the hospital and his mother Vera had seen him naked. Pat, who must have been a kind and generous woman, started caring for Tony. When her chauffeur retired Tony took on the job of driving her everywhere. And she did go everywhere. In those days *Coronation Street* stars got a reasonable salary but the real money came from public appearances. Pat took all the public appearances she was offered and for a few years she and Tony drove all over Britain between one PA and another. Tony would often sleep while she was working in the theatre. After the show she would fall alseep on the back seat of the car and he would drive off from Newcastle to Cardiff or some other long distance so she could open a supermarket, or give a speech at a lunch.

Of course Pat and Tony fell in love. They had always enjoyed one another's company, now both were lonely and needed support. In *Stroll On* Tony reports delightedly that sex, which had worried him all through his time in hospital, was no longer a problem. Bob Booth, Tony's brother, came home to live with Vera because his marriage had broken up and Tony began to live full time with Pat in Cheshire.

James Robinson, who has now lived at number 14 Ferndale Road for close on seventy years, said the most amazing event the street ever witnessed was the day Tony Booth brought Pat Phoenix to visit his mum Vera at number 15. Vera was decorating the front parlour, the bay-windowed room she was so proud of. The car drew up, Tony and Pat got out. Tony introduced Pat Phoenix, one of the most famous women in England, to Vera. Pat gave Vera a hug, took off her jacket and began to help with the decorating.

Cherie and Tony's budding romance was subjected to a test that two less suited, ambitious people may not have withstood. According to Irvine, only one of his pupils – the academic Cherie or the charming Tony – could stay on at 2 Crown Office Row. 'Both were my pupils. Both are highly intelligent. She had been very diligent at LSE when she came top of the Bar Finals, a combination of high ability and industry. Tony obviously enjoyed himself more at university, but he was a lawyer of the highest intelligence. He has a remarkable ability to sift through a mass of material, define issues and come up with the answers.'

However, when asked why Tony was chosen over Cherie, who had after all come top in the Bar exams, Derry Irvine avoided the issue: 'They are an extremely able couple. She chose toward the end of her pupillage to accept an offer from another Chambers. I was not the head of Chambers. She decided to take a bird in the hand. She had to calculate what was best for her.'

Michael Burton, who was later Head of Chambers and is now a High Court Judge, said 'We always did what he [Irvine] said in relation to his pupils and he did not recommend taking them both, he only recommended Tony.' This seems to imply that he could perhaps have taken them both on but chose a different outcome.

In 1975, the year Tony Blair met Cherie Booth, 1,002 people were called to the Bar in England and Wales: 890 of them were male and only 112 female. There were 637 Members of Parliament elected at the 1979 election and only nineteen of them were women. Today males and females are called to the Bar in almost equal numbers and 108 Westminster MPs are female. A third of the cabinet in Tony Blair's second administration are women. In the mid-1970s, however smart and clever she was believed to be, the chances of Cherie being chosen for anything before the charismatic Tony were slim. There were still three years to go before the Equal Pay Act and four years before the first female Prime Minister.

On the surface, at least, Cherie should have been a better choice as a pupil than Tony. Derry Irvine rang his friend Michael Beloff and said Cherie was in the set. 'He asked me: "Can you do something for her?"' says Beloff, 'She came to see me. No false modesty, sold herself.' But it didn't work out. No one is quite sure why.

So Derry Irvine tried another friend.

These days Fredric Reynold QC is a distinguished senior barrister. He's at Old Square Chambers, a traditional set which specializes in employment, trade union and public law. The building backs on to the quiet peaceful gardens of Gray's Inn, and has the studious feel of an Oxford college. Next door through an archway in the old brick wall you can see the modern steel nameplate of Matrix, the new chambers specializing in human rights where Cherie Booth QC works. Today Reynold and Booth are close friends who often lunch together. They met in 1977. 'One summer's day I was rung by Derry Irvine who was a rising junior specializing in the same areas as me. We worked together sometimes. He asked if he could come over for a chat. He was concerned about finding a home for one of his pupils. He had two excellent pupils, one male and one female.'

They were of course Blair and Booth. Irvine was trying to find a home for Cherie. 'He spent a long time singing her praises, explaining her strengths. I recall mildly asking if there were any drawbacks or deficiencies in this lady's formidable repertoire of gifts. Derry said he had some reservations about her handwriting and that from time to time her punctuality left something to be desired, but we both agreed these were small disadvantages and that her attributes and qualities outweighed them.' Fredric Reynold agreed to see Cherie and liked her immediately. 'She had all the spontaneous artlessness of a twenty-two-year-old. I spoke to our Head of Chambers David McNeil and said I was impressed by her academic record. Her CV was excellent and she had a scholarship from Lincoln's Inn.' McNeil was impressed with her too and within a week Cherie was hired. Reynold said: 'It wouldn't happen now. The route she took to us was via networking. Derry had pushed the boat out for her. That was how things were done in those days.'

Cherie was an immediate success at her new chambers: 'She was, to use that appalling cliché, very focused. I liked her spontaneity. She said what she thought without any artifice. She had charm, a natural charm. She dealt with questions in a very focused way,' says Reynold.

It wasn't long before everyone in the chambers discovered that Cherie was courting. Her young man, Tony Blair, used to be waiting for her outside the front door at the end of the working day.

This must have been a key point in Cherie's development, when she saw demonstrated for the first time that there were other tools in the tool cupboard, tools that some people seemed to value more than intelligence and hard work. Charm was one of them, but it was even more important to be male and middle-class.

In Britain in the 1970s the only sure way for a woman to get to the top was to marry a man who was already on his way there. So the question of Cherie's individual abilities are irrelevant; the important fact is that she and Tony got together. Two young people who combined the talents of Tony Blair and Cherie Booth made a formidable team, whether they knew it yet or not.

Derry Irvine observed that they were good together: 'They share many values, but there's no question, as sometimes happens with two highly intelligent people, that their life is a battle of wits. They are relaxed together. She is more narrowly professional. Tony paints across a very broad canvas. He'd be interested to talk about practically anything. Tony relishes knowing people from all walks of life, is more sociable than he might appear. I'm not suggesting Cherie doesn't as well but she is a specialist and he is a generalist.'

Tony and Cherie's relationship developed as they both pursued their legal careers. They both shared rented flats with friends in London. Cherie shared with Maggie Rae, another lawyer who these days is a divorce specialist often to be heard dispensing wise advice on Radio Four consumer programmes and who is married to Alan Howarth, secretary of the Parliamentary Labour Party. Tony shared a flat with Charles Falconer, who has been at his side ever since. (He was the ill-fated Dome Minister in the first Blair administration and promoted to Housing Minister in the 2001 government, having been given a peerage by Blair in 1997.)

In the summer of 1977, when Tony and Cherie had been together for two years they rented a holiday flat in Italy. She liked him as a friend and enjoyed the fun and good times he brought her. She was still uncertain that she wanted to spend the rest of her life with him. Cherie knew more than most people about failed marriages. Her mother had been dumped in an unfamiliar town with two young children when Tony Booth walked out on her. She had spent fifteen years living with her mother-in-law before she managed to get a small council flat of her own. Cherie had every reason to be cautious about potential marriage partners.

Tony had made up his mind. He knew what he wanted with certainty.

'I'd come to the complete conviction in my own mind that this was the person I wanted to marry. I kept thinking about it, I was very nervous and then quite near the end of the fortnight I suddenly thought: "Right, it's now or never."'

Anthony Charles Lynton Blair asked Cherie Booth to marry him and, overcoming her reservations, she agreed.

Tony Booth was told of his eldest daughter's decision and rang his fifth daughter Lauren to tell her the news: 'Jeez! Have you heard? Cherie's marrying a Tory.' The line might have come straight out of *Till Death Us Do Part*. Tony Blair was a good-looking white boy who'd been to Oxford and was well on his way to becoming a London barrister. He'd done Booth's daughter out of a top job, and then he had persuaded her to marry him.

In Tony Booth's eyes only Tories behaved like that.

Tony Blair married Cherie Booth on Saturday 29 March 1980 in the Chapel of St John's College, Oxford, where six years earlier he had been confirmed as a member of the Church of England. He was 26. She was 25.

Before the wedding, Cherie and Tony went to Oxford to visit Anthony Phillips, the chaplain whom Tony had befriended during his student years. Phillips knew straight away they were suited to one another. 'They were a very serious young couple, very much in love.' He had no doubts about their devotion to each other. 'They stood out because they were so devoted to each other and so devout in their Christianity.'

Cherie probably chose Oxford for her wedding rather than her home town of Crosby because her mother was now an Oxford resident. Gale, who had no choice but to stay at Ferndale Road while her girls were growing up, left Liverpool very soon after Lyndsey left school. After fifteen years sharing her mother-in-law's terraced house with assorted Booth relations when they were down on their luck, she had at long last been able to start a life on her own. She applied for a transfer from Lewises in Liverpool where she worked in the travel agency and was moved to the Oxford branch. In 1980 Gale was living in rented accommodation in Sidney Street and Cherie, who was at this time sharing a London flat with Maggie Rae, gave her mother's Oxford address on her marriage certificate.

According to Anthony Phillips, the Blair wedding was like hundreds of others he has conducted. 'I had no idea I was marrying a future Prime Minister. They were perfectly ordinary people.' The chapel of St John's is not spacious so the congregation was relatively small. Cherie's larger-than-life father Tony Booth was not present because he was still in hospital. Cherie wore a Liberty dress and Derry Irvine gave a speech on Tony Booth's behalf. He explained how he had taken Tony and Cherie to lunch at Luigi's, where they became so interested in each other that he felt like a bit of a gooseberry and had to leave. He said that he felt that in the lives of this young couple he had played the part of 'Cupid QC'.

Anthony Phillips kept the address he gave at Tony and Cherie's wedding and when the Blairs made the move to Downing Street he wrote to Cherie and offered her his thoughts on her wedding day. She wrote back to say that she was delighted to have a copy of the speech and that she tried to live by his words.

> There are three things which are too wondrous for me, yea, four which I know what.
> The way of the eagle in the air, the way of a serpent upon a rock; the way of a ship in the midst of the sea, and the way of a man with a maid.

This was the text around which Phillips wrote his remarks: Proverbs 30, verses 18 and 19. He did not choose it specially for the Blairs. It is one he's used frequently for weddings over the years, hoping that it draws attention to the mystery of life for newlyweds. Why do eagles soar without flapping their wings? How do snakes travel across the earth? How do ships sail through the ocean, and how do people choose their life's partner? These were great mysteries and beyond the comprehension of the ancient Egyptians. What makes a man or woman fall in love with one person rather than another? Anthony Phillips invites the newlyweds to think about the mystery of why they chose each other.

Tony Blair has certainly thought about this a lot. Whenever he is asked about Cherie, he stresses how important their relationship is to his work as Prime Minister, to everything he does in his life. There is no doubting his dependence on her. Looking at the two of them together it is not really possible to believe that either could have made it to the top without the other. Twenty years after their marriage they have become inseparable in the public's perception.

That March day in Oxford in 1980 both were buying into a mutual support system which is unique amongst even the most modern of marriages and even more unique in couples in the public eye. It is not unusual for a man to marry a clever woman who will run his business, grow his fortune or develop his career, but wives like these usually remain silent and unacknowledged while the male is the public face of the business partnership. It is becoming more common today for the wife to be the partner who enjoys public success while her husband runs the household and spends more time with the children. However, measured and equal development like the Blairs', with each partner advancing and playing a part in the other's success, is still very rare.

Observers throughout Cherie Booth's life always mention her appreciation of her own worth, not in a pompous or puffed up way, more a certainty of what she wanted to do and what she believed in. She went into her marriage confident that she would play an equal part with her husband.

Cherie Booth walked down the aisle of St John's College chapel on the last Saturday in March 1980 in a conventional bridal gown. They were, said the man who married them, just an ordinary couple. Their future together was to be far from ordinary.

Seven

MAKING IT TOGETHER

The Blairs had a short honeymoon in Tuscany. They came back to London in the spring of 1980 to begin not only their married life but their political life together.

In the year following the wedding, Tony changed to a new set of chambers. The ambitious Derry Irvine moved out of Crown Office Row and took his former pupil Tony Blair with him. There had been an instant bonding between the two, and it has lasted till this day. Irvine still remains one of the closest people to Blair, staying on for a second term as Lord Chancellor despite several campaigns against him in the press on account of his perceived arrogance and his exclusive style

In 1981 Irvine and Blair moved to 1 Harcourt Buildings. Irvine is still in the same chambers today but it has moved again to 11 Kings Bench Walk.

Cherie was to stay with Fredric Reynold for over a decade. The chambers became well known when they were joined by the flamboyant George Carman QC not long after Cherie returned from her honeymoon.

The Blairs had returned to England having boosted each other's interest in party politics. Both had been active in their respective local branches in the years when they were going out together. Cherie had been a school governor in St John's Wood, north London, and Tony had taken various jobs on his local party executive. Now they were about to join their local branch together for the first time. They had revealed to each other, but not yet to the outside world, that they shared ambitions to become Labour Members of Parliament. In Cherie's case it just

84

wouldn't have been possible for her to join anything but the Labour Party. Tony was different. He didn't have a strong idealistic connection to any party, and wanted to use politics to promote his own ideas for improving society.

Cherie had joined the Labour Party while she was still at school through Dr and Mrs Speight, a Quaker couple who were leading lights in the United Nations Association in Crosby. Crosby was a solidly Tory town where right-wing views predominated. There was even a small cell of the National Front active in Waterloo in the 1970s. The Speights were passionate anti-racists with internationalist views which appealed to young left-wingers like Cherie. Jim Hulligan, who was also a member, remembers Cherie as moderately left of centre, quiet, and a good listener.

Tony Blair's political background was more right wing. He had been to a public school and Oxford. His father had been a Conservative councillor. With his charming demeanour and his middle-class accent he looked and sounded like a young Conservative. But in 1975 Tony Blair had joined the Labour Party. He too was moderately left of centre. Charles Falconer, who had known Blair at school and then ran into him again when they found themselves working in different Chambers but in the same building in the Temple, says that Oxford had changed Blair: 'As a schoolboy he had been a very attractive, strong character, intelligent but not preoccupied with the concerns he had when he came down from Oxford. He came away more genuinely altruistic than anybody I knew. He had a much more thought out, much less fashionable view of things than the people around him. In the 1970s there were lots of tempting options for people wanting to make a difference, far left politics were prevalent among many of us. Tony always knew it was a dead end.'

When the political hopefuls arrived back from Tuscany they stayed for a few months in the flat which Cherie as a single girl had shared with Maggie Rae. Eventually they found a house just a couple of blocks away. They joined the Queensbridge Road branch of the Hackney Labour Party and started building up a circle of friends who have stayed close to them to this day.

Their first home together was 59 Mapledene Road, London E8, in today's estate agent's speak 'a well presented three bedroom, three-storey, Victorian mid-terrace house. Period features include sash windows, high coved ceilings and centre roses. Much sought after location being in the London Fields conservation area. Guide price £320,000.'

When the Blairs bought number 59, Hackney was a mixed area and their street, surrounded by 1960s and 1970s tower blocks and just down from Hoxton market, was affordable as starter homes for young professionals. 'They sanded the floors, restored the original features and filled them up with Habitat furniture,' said a less upwardly mobile neighbour of the time. In the 1980s young middle-class couples turned their backs on new building. The horrors of the 1960s and 1970s were everywhere, and skilfully reclaimed Victorian houses were still affordable status symbols.

About the same time as the Blairs arrived in Mapledene Road, Barry Cox and his wife moved next door to number 57. Cox is a television producer and director who worked at Thames Television on the *This Week* programme with Jonathan Dimbleby and David Elstein, later moving to London Weekend Television to climb the executive tree. During the ITV franchise war in 1990 he was golden handcuffed to LWT who won back their franchise. As a result most of their executives became very rich and Cox became a millionaire. In 1994 he was the key fundraiser in Blair's brief campaign to become Labour leader. He is still a close friend and entertains Tony and Cherie in his homes in Richmond and in France. Number 57 Mapledene Road is still in the Cox family.

The Queensbridge Road branch of the Hackney South Labour Party was as mixed as the housing. This was the constituency where the *Militant* newspaper was printed, and party membership ranged from bus conductors to barristers. The local MP, Ron Brown, brother of the more famous George, was on the right of the party. A member at the time says that the party locally was 'split, riven with strife'. There was a war on and some party members devoted their lives to the bitter fighting between left and right. Tony Blair and Cherie Booth supported Ron Brown throughout. Not long after the Limehouse declaration and the formation of the SDP in 1981 Brown defected, leaving the Blairs and others like them hurt and embarrassed.

Tony and Cherie were both of the 'soft left', as the middle ground was called in those days, with Cherie marginally more to the left than Tony. In meetings of the General Management Committee she would play to the left, but not be of it. Neither she nor Tony would get involved in the party bickering. A party member observed: 'I always thought they were remarkable for the way they rose above that and they didn't get involved. Cherie was temperamentally more drawn by leftishness. Her heart-strings were pulled by rhetoric, equality for the working class, that sort of thing. After all, she came from that background herself.'

Tony and Cherie were the most obviously bourgeois couple in the Hackney South party. They were young, good looking, very bright, very amiable. The two of them were seen and talked about by others as the up-and-coming couple. It was known that both Tony and Cherie were looking for a seat: neither made any secret of it. They were Mr and Mrs Very Ambitious But Nice. This was a new characteristic in a party where it had long been a tradition for people modestly to refuse to put themselves forward but to acquiesce graciously when their colleagues nominated them. Tony and Cherie had always been frank about their ambitions.

While the Blairs were setting themselves up in Hackney, Jim Callaghan was just resigning as leader of the Labour Party. He was replaced by Michael Foot, chosen by a ballot of Labour Members of Parliament. It was to be the last time MPs had this power. At the party conference in the autumn it was decided to change the system, but the problem was: to what? 'Who should elect the Party leader?' was the first issue Tony and Cherie were involved in at a meeting of their local party. There was to be a special conference at Wembley in the new year to vote for a new way of selecting the leader. Hackney South Labour Party debated two alternatives, 'an electoral college', which was supported by people on the left, and 'one member one vote', which won the support of the right. Election by MPs was not even discussed. Both Blairs opted for one member one vote, but they were outvoted. Callaghan accepted the principle of an electoral college and abandoned the right of MPs to select the leader in a meeting with trade union leaders at Bishop's Stortford. This then had to be ratified. At the conference in January 1981 at Wembley the Labour Party nationally also threw out the idea and opted for an electoral college. It would take another thirteen years before OMOV (One Member One Vote) replaced it, when John Smith pushed through change with the help of John Prescott at the 1994 party conference.

Within months of their arrival in Hackney, Tony and Cherie had both been elected to the General Management Committee of the party. Tony beat a strong left-winger by two votes and became Ward Secretary. Party members claim to have spotted a glint of ambition in his eye even at this level.

People who were party members at the time and became friends of Tony have remained friends to this day and many of them are firmly inside the Blair tent. In addition to the Coxes next door, Maggie Rae and her partner (now husband Alan Howarth) are perhaps the closest. Howarth has been Secretary of the Labour Party for years. Mark Jones, the new Curator of the Victoria and Albert museum and the man who founded the National Museum in Scotland, was a neighbour and party member. Charles Clarke, Blair-appointed Chairman of the Labour Party following the 2001 General Election and member of the cabinet, shared a garden fence with the Blairs. John Lloyd of the *New Statesman* and Baroness Glenys Thornton, former secretary of the Fabian Society and the woman charged with making all-women shortlists of candidates work in the 1997 election, were Hackney neighbours who have stayed in touch.

Blair didn't tell his Hackney friends at the time, but while they were all fighting the good fight at local level, as Derry Irvine's sidekick, Tony was advising the Labour Party professionally on how to deal with Militant.

Some of the Hackney party remember visiting the Blairs at home: 'I used to go round there a bit. I met Derry Irvine round there once. Tony and Cherie were always bright. I never saw them out of sorts with each other. They would always bicker a bit, but usually amiably. It was after all the early years of their marriage. They were always hospitable, they always listened. What is always said about Tony is that he listens, and he would often listen to Cherie. Cherie would talk more than him.

'Sometimes he seemed affectionately exasperated with her when she was putting her points. "Ah well, Cherie…" he would begin an explanation of something he didn't think possible.'

Of course they were in theory on the same footing. Both of them were young bright barristers who wanted to be MPs. A male friend said that he always thought that Tony would get a seat and Cherie might take a back seat. Of course it was much harder for women to get selected for safe seats in the early 1980s, when there were only nineteen females out of 650 MPs. It would have been entirely normal for a couple to start out as equals and then for the relationship to change when children arrived and the woman found herself with much more domestic responsibility. 'Cherie would have made a very good MP. She would have made a very good minister, but Tony had the harder edge although he is deemed the softer person.'

Both Blairs began to search for seats. In 1981 the Conservative MP for Crosby Sir Graham Page died. It was announced that Shirley Williams, member of the Gang of Four and freshly defected from the Labour Party, would stand for the SDP. Cherie Booth was upset: 'I was particularly keen on Shirley Williams as she was a Catholic and a woman who had made her name politically. I felt let down when she defected to the SDP and in fact decided to throw my hat in the ring to be the candidate in Crosby in 1981 when she stood there. I was really looking in the south-east at the time because Tony was looking in the north, but I felt outraged that she was going to stand in Crosby, my home town – I actually went up and addressed a meeting, but didn't get the nomination.'

Cherie got onto the shortlist for Crosby. Jim Hulligan Chair of the Victoria Ward at the time remembers, that she had at least two nominations. One from his ward and the other from NUPE, the National Union of Public Employees. There were five on the shortlist and Cherie was the only woman. Jim said she gave an excellent speech and he supported her, but the party wanted someone local. Because she was now a London barrister, Cherie, who had spent pretty much her whole life in Crosby, was not now local enough. And of course she was a woman and it was still very hard indeed for women to get chosen for a high-profile seat. The party selected John Backhouse, a young maths teacher, who made little impression on the electorate, came in a poor third and has never been heard of since.

Outside the door during the selection conference, hoping to be invited in to hear the speeches, stood Tony Booth, nervously supporting his eldest daughter. He promised the local party all sorts of help if Cherie were chosen. Tony Booth could muster an army of out-of-work theatricals to canvass for the candidate. Booth kept his promise even though the candidate was John Backhouse. He came along with Pat Phoenix and chaired a big public meeting. But the seat was won by Shirley Williams with a huge swing to the SDP.

Over the next couple of years Cherie was to rely on Tony Booth for the first time in her life. Booth and his partner Pat Phoenix were a big draw card for Labour voters and turned up to give their support every time Cherie or Tony became a candidate.

Tony Blair tried and failed to get on the shortlist for two seats in the north, Middlesbrough and Teesside Thornaby. Stuart Bell had the Middlesbrough seat sewn up with the unions and Frank Griffiths got the Thornaby nomination. Both had worked hard on their local connections and Blair was seen as an outsider and a southerner to boot.

Back in London, the Blairs made an odd one-off joint attempt to get elected as a Hackney Councillor. There was a vote to choose three candidates for the Queensbridge ward. Tony put himself forward, but because he had a court case to deal with Cherie got up in the selection meeting and spoke on his behalf. It was an unsuccessful double act. People at the meeting felt that if Tony wanted to be a councillor he should have managed to turn up for his selection meeting.

Ronald Bell, the Conservative MP for Beaconsfield, died in February 1982. It looked like another chance of a seat for the Social Democrats. A huge swing had given Shirley Williams Crosby and Roy Jenkins won Hillhead in the run-up to Beaconsfield. All the interest in Beaconsfield was in the new kind of two-party race, Conservatives against Social Democrats. There was very little interest in who the Labour Party chose as their candidate. It was the first chance for Tony Blair. The local Labour Party in Beaconsfield loved him. He was young and good looking and came across as sincere and honest. But the campaign was totally overshadowed by international events. Blair was chosen as the Labour candidate on the first of April. Argentina invaded the Falkland Islands less than twenty-four hours later. Tony Blair was conscientious about his candidacy and meticulously toed the party line and had plenty of senior Labour figures to canvass for him (including Michael Foot, John Smith, Roy Hattersley and Neil Kinnock). There were also a couple of public appearances by the Booth relations as supporting stars on the stump. Tony Booth and Pat Phoenix came together to Beaconsfield to support the son-in-law's first outing as a candidate. They did their bit in Beaconsfield, having their photo taken and going door to door with the candidate. The part of candidate's wife was played by Mrs Cherie Blair.

Back in 1982 the Labour Party believed that if at all possible candidates should display wives and families to sing their praises and by their very presence demonstrate the candidates' 'normality', as Norman Tebbit was to put it nearly twenty years later. The biggest fights in the Mitchell family were always a few weeks before General Elections when Candidate Mitchell would demand that wife and badly behaved children should assemble smiling and well-dressed to be photographed for his election leaflet. We all hated the idea and there would be tears and squabbling for days. Eventually a soft focus shot of a sullen family would be approved by someone in the regional Labour Party office. I was expected to endorse my husband with a glowing paragraph outlining his virtues. No matter what vitriol poured from my pen, it was turned into a hymn of praise.

Mrs Cherie Blair added her voice to her husband's leaflet and was much better than I was at getting her own point across. 'As a member for ten years I believe that only the Labour Party shows real concern for the welfare of women today. At a time of economic recession women are often the first casualties, not only in terms of employment – but also because the burden of public spending cuts falls more heavily on them.'

The war in the Falklands improved the Conservative government's standing enormously, and Tory candidate Tim Smith won Beaconsfield from Paul Tyler, the Liberal/SDP Alliance candidate. Tony Blair got 3,886 votes and lost his deposit.

It was Cherie's turn next. In the lead-up to the 1983 General Election, the Chairman of Thanet North Labour Party, Reg Ward, was on the lookout for a woman to put on his shortlist. His wife Mary and other women in the local party thought it would be good to have at least one woman on the shortlist. Thanet North wasn't a winnable seat as the Conservative MP William Rees-Davies had a big majority, so up-and-coming stars were not an option. Reg had asked a few people to consider Thanet and been turned down. He remembers chatting with Tessa Blackstone, now Baroness Blackstone, the Arts Minister: she declined to put her name forward.

Reg Ward, who was a member of EETPU (the electricians' and plumbers' trade union) and a friend of Ron Hayward, was often in and around Transport House (then Labour Party headquarters). A lot of plotting was done in the pub across the road.

Someone from the old Agents Department asked Reg if he knew a bright young barrister called Cherie Booth who was hunting for a seat. Reg was apprehensive but he got in touch. The party had once got Mrs Connor, wife of the acerbic *Daily Mirror* columnist Cassandra, to come to a selection meeting and it had been a disaster.

Cherie went down to Thanet for a selection meeting on a weekend afternoon. She went alone and joined three male hopefuls in a quest for a hopeless seat. 'A missionary fight, that's what we call it. You've got to go in for it with missionary zeal,' says Reg, chairman that afternoon. The candidates each spoke for fifteen minutes and then there were ten minutes for questions from the members of the General Management Committee. 'It was quite clear Cherie had prepared herself well. She had got some research done, and she put it over clearly and precisely. Then came the first ballot. She won outright. No more ballots needed. Cherie Booth was selected as the Thanet North Labour candidate for the 1983 General Election.' Candidate Cherie was congratulated by her new party and put on the train back to London.

At some stage – and it's impossible to be certain when (Reg Ward is clear that they didn't know when they selected her) – the local party discovered or were told that Cherie was Tony Booth's daughter. One of the main problems worrying local Labour Parties in the run-up to the 1983 election was the new prominence of the fledgling SDP who had won two high-profile by-elections. Reg found out that the SDP had planned a major meeting in Margate on 28 April, about two months before the election. When Cherie Booth came down for a planning meeting Reg put forward the idea that Labour would hold a meeting on the same night with stars on the platform who could outshine Roy Jenkins. The Labour Party booked Margate Town Hall and announced that Tony Benn (at that time the most charismatic Labour politician in the land), the candidate and the candidate's father would be on the platform. Tony Booth was an enormous draw card even in posh Margate. The hall was packed. Two hundred extra people listened to the speeches on loudspeakers outside the hall. Roy Jenkins and the SDP were roundly defeated, for one night only. In the audience, definitely taking a back seat while his wife had her first taste of stardom, was the candidate's husband Tony Blair.

Reg Ward says that Tony Blair was sometimes a bit of a nuisance and had to be put in his place. During the election and the run-up to it when Cherie was in Thanet she stayed in the Ward's modest back bedroom. Tony would come down to visit occasionally and the Blairs and the Wards would sit talking politics over the dinner table, but Tony was always interrupting. 'The bloody candidate's spouse kept butting in. Eventually, I turned and said to him "I'm talking to the candidate. She's the candidate. You're not."' Reg says his wife, who was a diplomat and realized the difficulties of the situation, took Tony out to the kitchen to do the dishes.

Not long after Cherie was selected, the Conservative MP William Rees-Davies, another barrister whom Cherie was looking forward to challenging, was de-selected by his local party. Rees-Davies, who'd lost an arm in the war, was nicknamed locally 'the one-armed bandit'. He was suspected of being involved in a corruption scandal and the Tories replaced him with a children's TV programme producer from Thames Television named Roger Gale, who had unsuccessfully stood for Birmingham Northfield in 1979.

Cherie fought the election as a traditional left-winger, a supporter of *Tribune*. She took a standard anti-bomb line based on creating more work for people. There was nothing extreme about her views and pronouncements. Before the 1997 election Peter Hitchens, then of the *Daily Express*, started a campaign to find out what he called 'the real truth' about Cherie. He was looking for evidence of an extreme past like her father's. He uncovered nothing, but it seems he worried Blair's office a good deal.

While I was interviewing him for this book, Reg Ward reached over to his bookshelf and produced John Rentoul's and Jon Sopel's biographies of Blair. Both were signed with grateful thanks from the new Prime Minister and his wife. When Hitchens was searching in Thanet, Reg was warned by someone in the leader's office to make sure Hitchens was put off the scent. There are two Hitchens brothers – Christopher is a left-winger while Peter is of the right – and for a moment Reg thought he was talking to Christopher, but warnings from London made the position clear. Why Blair's team thought it was necessary to mislead Hitchens when there was nothing to hide about Cherie's past is unclear, but better to be safe than sorry. The incident marked the way Alastair Campbell and his team would manage Tony and Cherie and their public exposure in the future. Reg did what he was asked to do and was less than helpful to Peter Hitchens when he made the journey down to Thanet. After the election the autographed books arrived along with a note of grateful thanks from Cherie at her chambers.

Reg Ward feels he and his wife taught Cherie a lot. Her outfits had needed a bit of attention. 'She wasn't too particular about her appearance. She wore severe clothes. Let's just say she hadn't got her best coat on when she came here. My wife had a discreet word with her. Gave her a hint. "Don't play the market down," she said. "Just because we're Labour doesn't mean we can't be well turned out." Cherie got the message.

The Wards also quickly discovered that Cherie was a serious Roman Catholic. 'When she first came here she asked us if we would mind if she got up and went to church on Sunday mornings. Of course, we said not. She had her own key so she was free to come and go as she pleased. Off she would go every Sunday and not get back till we had eaten our breakfast. She just made her own later. Toast and marmalade.'

It was a different story on weekdays. Reg was up every morning and off to the office at 7.30. His wife left at 8.30 because she was a teacher. Cherie, whose husband has described her as needing a nuclear explosion to wake her, was left sleeping soundly until sometime mid-morning, when she would meet her agent Frank Green and do some canvassing.

As the election drew near Tony Blair felt depressed about the way things had turned out. Unless there was an unexpected revolution Cherie wouldn't be an MP after the election but she would have gained valuable experience as a candidate. His only role was 'spouse of a Labour candidate', and from what he had learned in Thanet North, it was strictly a non-speaking part.

On Monday 9 May 1983 Margaret Thatcher announced that the election would be held thirty days later on 9 June. There were few seats left without a Labour candidate, but Sedgefield in County Durham was one. The constituency had been assembled from chunks of other seats in the latest boundary reorganization. Left-winger Les Huckfield, who had been the MP for Nuneaton, had been courting the Sedgefield party and had several nominations. Tony Blair decided it was worth a trip to the north to look for a nomination.

Labour candidates in the 1980s went round collecting nominations from wards and branches, affiliated organizations and trade unions. At the time Bryan Gould and I were working for the Thames Television current affairs programme *TV Eye*. Bryan, who had been defeated in Southampton in 1979, was for a long time in the same position as Blair, searching for a seat. On unproductive afternoons in the office we would ring round branch secretaries and affiliated organizations in winnable seats (Warrington was one) to see whether there was a chance Bryan could get some nominations. Eventually he was selected for the safe outer London seat, Dagenham. He had few nominations and had perhaps only been there once. The selection was on a Saturday. Bryan got off a plane from a filming trip to Japan and went straight to Dagenham for the selection conference. He won. Of course Bryan was a retread and well known, which Blair was not, but it was certainly not unheard of for a promising candidate to come through the middle and defeat people who had been soliciting nominations for weeks.

One man was really responsible for Tony Blair becoming the Labour candidate for Sedgefield: John Burton, who was the first person in the constituency to get to know him, and remains his agent to this day. Burton identifies, as so many others have done meeting him for the first time, that Tony was different from other hopefuls. He had new ideas and he wanted to change the Labour Party. 'He rang me up because we were the last seat to pick a candidate. He hadn't been successful at all but he managed to get a list of secretaries of the local wards and he saw that Trimdon village hadn't nominated anyone. He asked if he could come to see me and I told him we were meeting in my house the next evening. There were five of us and I told him to pop along. He's told me since that he hadn't seen Cherie for quite a long time and he nearly didn't come. He thought he wouldn't be successful so he tried to ring me back to tell me he wasn't coming, but he dialled the wrong number and didn't get through.

'So in the end he turned up and we were watching the final of the European Cup-Winners Cup, Aberdeen versus Real Madrid. We had a wine box or some beer and I said 'sit down and have a drink.' Of course it went to full time. It went extra time and penalties. He sat there. He thought, coming from the London Labour Party where people were throwing each other off balconies, and that kind of thing, we appeared to be quite normal because he could see we preferred football to politics. Eventually we got round to the politics.

'There was something about him – you can't put your finger on it. You can talk about charisma, which was definitely there, but he wasn't just giving us the answers that you normally get. If I want to get a nomination and I come to your house I will tell you what you want to hear, but he didn't sound like that. He wasn't giving us Labour Party policy, he was giving us his beliefs that the Labour Party had to change. It had to become a party of mass membership. He didn't agree with unilateral nuclear disarmament, which was Labour Party policy and was a disaster which lost us the election. He believed we should be playing a more central part in Europe. Actually taking part in the discussions and not sitting on the outside and moaning about things. This was someone who was trying to get us to support him but wasn't telling us what the Labour Party was supposed to be saying and I think that impressed everybody in the room.'

John Burtons' wife Lily was also present that famous evening. 'I remember John saying to Tony 'Do you really want this?' and he said yes he really did. John said 'Well, we will work for you.'

'We really didn't have a chance to get him the nomination.' says John, 'we were five blokes sitting in a room and then we went off and tried to get people to support the idea, and then I went to the shortlisting meeting and he didn't get on the shortlist because the left rigged it for Les Huckfield. Of course you keep off anyone who is a threat.

The next night I went to a new part of the constituency where I had been to grammar school and some of the constituents I recognised, and two or three of them were related to Lily. Our local councillors were there and one or two people that I had played football with were there. When it came to Tony Blair's name being added to the shortlist I stood up and explained what I wanted to do. I suppose these people thought if John is supporting him we will not accept this short list. We will add someone to it. He got added by 42 votes to 41, and he is Prime Minister because of that. The three tellers all got different figures so there was a recount. It was amazing that he got selected. Roy Hattersley thought at the time that it was the Trade Union movement that had done it. It wasn't. It was five people going out and seeing people and getting all the support they could.'

Because he hadn't expected to get so far, Tony Blair had turned up in Trimdon without even a toothbrush, let alone a CV. His new best friend John Burton got someone to type something up from handwritten notes made by Tony Blair. Under the heading 'Family' he had written:

> I am married to Cherie Booth who was born and bred in Liverpool. Cherie is now a barrister (having come top in the professional exams in 1976 for the whole country). She specialises in childcare and adoption work. Cherie's father is the actor Anthony Booth of 'Till Death Us Do Part' fame. Anthony and Pat Phoenix from 'Coronation Street' both came to canvass for me when I previously stood for parliament and would happily do so again. Cherie and I as yet have no children. I have always wanted to come back to the North East to represent the community here. I would of course live in the constituency if selected and I would be a full time MP. Cherie's work, unlike mine, could transfer to the north.

It seems unlikely that Tony Blair had consulted the candidate for Thanet North about her future plans when he made the promise that she would in future conduct her business from Sedgefield.

Of course she was never asked to. He wouldn't have dared. Tony omitted to mention on his CV that his wife was also a candidate in the coming election. Whatever else they were up for, the idea of wives who were candidates in their own right was not something you boasted about in the north in 1983.

On Friday 20 May Tony Blair was selected on the fifth ballot as the Labour candidate for Sedgefield. As soon as he could he phoned Cherie at Reg Ward's home. 'She was sitting right here where I am now,' said Reg, leaning on his desk: 'When he told her that he had won she let out a great whoop of joy. Of course she knew he was on to a winner and their lives were going to change for ever.'

Lily Burton says that Tony couldn't go back to London after all that, and he had nowhere else to go: 'So he had to stay with us for three weeks before the election. Tony became part of the family and our dining room became campaign headquarters. It was exciting. He just settled in immediately. It was an interesting time, and he just made himself at home.'

In the event, the 1983 General Election brought contrasting fortunes for husband and wife:

Thanet North

Roger Gale (Con)	26,801
W. Macmillan (SDP)	12,256
Cherie Booth (Lab)	6,482
B .Dobing (BNP)	324

Sedgefield

Tony Blair (Lab)	21,401
T. Horton (Con)	13,120
D. Shand (SDP)	10,183
M. Logan-Salton (Ind)	298

Eight

WIFE OF THE
MP FOR SEDGEFIELD

On Wednesday 1 June 1983 Tony Blair received his first mention in the *Darlington Echo*, the daily newspaper serving the Sedgefield constituency. 'Guess Who's Down the Street?' asked the headline.

> *Coronation Street* sex bomb Pat Phoenix is right up Labour's street and maybe yours. The Street's famous worldly wise aunt plays out her working class Salford character for real when it comes to politics and it's not surprising.
>
> Cherie, the daughter of her actor boyfriend Tony Booth, is standing in the election and Cherie's husband, Labour man Tony Blair, is fighting it out for Sedgefield.
>
> Now Elsie Tanner fans in the mining community are to get some sound election advice from glamorous gran Pat when she joins Tony on his campaign in Sedgefield.
>
> And Tony Booth adding a bit of *Till Death Us Do Part* straight talking might be an ace in barrister Mr Blair's hand.
>
> 'She'll be a great help. Pat's very busy with commitments and her work for the Labour Party but she hopes to do some work with me here,' he said.
>
> 'She's a fantastic person. My wife Cherie and I see them regularly and Pat is as nice a person as she is on the programme,' said Mr Blair yesterday at a party for the over 60's club in Fishburn.
>
> Mr Blair, whose wife is standing for Thanet North, said the reception from the locals since he arrived had been fantastic. 'I see in the paper that the BBC says the Conservatives will win Sedgefield. That's rubbish and everybody who lives here knows it'.

When Tony Blair was elected to Parliament on 9 June 1983, the youngest member in the House of Commons at the age of thirty, he made a great leap forward in his career. Cherie Booth also acquired a new role. For better or for worse she had become 'The Member's Wife'. She had joined that unsung band of women, the wives of diplomats, doctors, politicians and priests who were expected in public and in private to spend a large chunk of time as unpaid helpmates to their spouses. It is hard to believe that less than twenty years ago a young woman could be asked to give so much in the service of someone else's career.

Today, a fifth of the membership of the House of Commons are women and perhaps half of those have husbands, so there are fifty or so men who are the partners of MPs. There are now women priests and vicars, and some of them have husbands. There are a few female diplomats who take their husbands with them on postings; the role of the GP has changed so much and there are so many women in the profession that no one expects their spouses to take a role in the local community.

Women haven't got equality at Westminster yet but perceptions have changed. In 2001 a young woman barrister with a politician partner does not feel that she has a compulsory second career in her husband's constituency. In all but the truest of blue seats voters understand if the Member's spouse is seldom seen in the constituency because he or she has a career of their own. Of course the locals want to know all about the MP's wife and family, and expect them to turn up on high days and holidays, but just about everyone accepts these days that one-career families where the wife stays at home and helps her husband with his profession are as rare as female MPs were in 1983, when just twenty-three of over six hundred MPs elected with Tony Blair were women.

My husband Austin Mitchell was elected to parliament in a by-election in April 1977 and my life changed for ever. Things had been working reasonably well. The village we lived in was about half-way between his workplace as a television journalist with Yorkshire TV in Leeds and mine as a television producer with Granada in Manchester. I had a daily nanny and my in-laws lived in a granny flat which was part of our house. The local school was at the bottom of our lane and although it was tough working, mothering and giving a hand occasionally to a couple of pensioners, it was nothing like as difficult as what happened next.

Just like the Blairs, everything in our lives changed suddenly. In February 1977 we were on holiday in the United States when we read in the *New York Times* that Anthony Crosland, the British Foreign Secretary and MP for Grimsby, had been taken ill and died. Just six weeks later, Austin was the MP for Grimsby.

It seemed just as sudden for the Blairs. Tony Blair had given up hope of finding a seat, safe or unsafe, for the 1983 election. He went to Sedgefield, the last Labour seat in England to choose a candidate, and put himself forward. He didn't really believe anything would come of it, but he thought there was nothing to be lost by trying. Four weeks later he was MP for Sedgefield.

In his application to be considered by the Sedgefield Labour Party, Tony Blair promised that he would live in the constituency, and that his wife Cherie could as well do her work as a barrister in the north of England as in London. It's doubtful that Cherie, who was in Thanet, was consulted about the wording. Austin Mitchell, fighting a much more marginal seat in a very fraught by-election, also promised at a public meeting with me sitting beside him on the platform, that if he won Grimsby we would come to live there with our kids.

Elections are exciting winner-takes-all contests, and in the heat of the race candidates believe all kinds of promises are necessary. We were outsiders who lived in Yorkshire. There was some graffiti on the road into Grimsby announcing 'Death to all Yorkies'. The Tory was a local man who was expected to win. The Labour majority was small and the Labour government, only eighteen months from its end, was unpopular. In those circumstances and looking back from the sunlit uplands of a new century it is possible to forgive Austin for making a promise that took no regard of my career or the kids and on which he hadn't bothered to consult me. The trouble was Austin felt he had to stick to his promise.

Tony Blair's promise to live seven days a week in the constituency was quietly forgotten. I imagine Cherie's reaction to life in the constituency with a husband absent in London was much the same as mine. The Blairs continued to live and work in London but faithfully made the 250-mile trip to Sedgefield just about every weekend. Whichever way they travelled – there was a choice of car, plane and train – they were committed to spending an extra full working day a week (eight hours or so) travelling back and forth to the constituency.

When Tony won Sedgefield Cherie may not have known it but she was pregnant. Reg Ward reckons Euan was a General Election baby conceived in Sedgefield the one weekend that the Thanet Labour candidate took leave to visit her husband. John Rentoul in his biography of Tony Blair points out that Blair was coy about his family in his CV: 'Cherie and I as yet have no children.' John Burton with a twinkle in his eye told me that after Tony was elected Cherie would come up and join him at the weekends: 'Of course he was down there during the week at Parliament and at the weekends they stayed with us until they found a house of their own. That was quite a long time, almost a year. My daughter gave her room up and she had to sleep on the floor in Jonathan my son's room.

Tony and Cherie had two single beds in the bedroom. Occasionally we found the two mattresses pushed together on the floor and the two single beds became a double bed.'

There was a fit of giggling then from both Burtons. Just like Reg Ward down in Thanet, they are claiming that Euan Blair is a real Sedgefield lad.

For Cherie this was the beginning of a decade of building up her career as a barrister, producing three babies at two-yearly intervals and travelling pretty much every weekend 250 miles north to do her duties as 'MP's wife' in her husband's constituency.

Life was much tougher for working women twenty-five years ago. Fredric Reynold, who worked with Cherie as one of her senior barristers during these years, told me that he thought she was disadvantaged as a woman barrister in the 1970s and 1980s. She was given a lot of work involving children and family law because solicitors in those days stereotyped women and the work that they could do. It was also argued that there were strong economic reasons not to have women barristers because clients would not like it. Cherie would have had even more problems if her interest had been in commercial or property or tax law where women were absolutely frowned upon. Cherie's younger sister Lyndsey, who followed Cherie's path to a legal career and who had a talent for shipping law, had great difficulties getting a place because of her gender. Cherie's real interest was in public law and employment law, the areas Reynold specialized in himself, and she worked as his junior on a number of cases.

He recalls: 'One case that eventually went to the House of Lords concerned the contractual rights of a member of a trade union. It was alleged by the Transport and General Workers Union that Apex had poached a number of their members. There was a Disputes Committee presided over by Joe Gormley set up under the TUC's arbitration procedures, and this committee decided that Apex had acted wrongly. They were told to give the members back and ensure they were transferred back to the T & G. One of these members was aggrieved. He wanted to stay in Apex and he challenged the rule that Apex could terminate his membership if it was necessary to comply with a decision of the TUC Disputes Committee. He brought an action and the case was heard by then Mr Justice Bingham later the Lord Chief Justice and now the senior Law Lord. He decided in favour of Apex. The case then went to the Court of Appeal. Lord Denning presided and by a majority of two to one they decided for the individual member. We appealed to the House of Lords on behalf of Apex and we won.

'Cherie had to do quite a lot of research for me in that case and her notes and the quality of her contribution was excellent. I remember her efforts also being praised by other counsel who had been brought in by the TUC and that counsel then became a Law Lord – Lord Saville who is now chairing the Londonderry Inquiry. He was very impressed with Cherie's note which dealt with the European law dimension to the case, and she played a very helpful part in that case.'

As if it wasn't enough being a full-time barrister, a mother and the wife of the MP for Sedgefield, Cherie kept her active interest in politics going for a few years after her marriage.

Cherie and Tony both joined the Labour Co-ordinating Committee. The LCC was originally set up in 1978 by supporters of Tony Benn. Michael Meacher was one of the moving forces. After the 1979 defeat, the Labour Co-ordinating Committee was the main group supporting the idea of an electoral college to choose the leader. Cherie and Tony were supporters of one member one vote. Cherie was more active than her husband and on the executive for a few years. The present Europe Minister Peter Hain met her there.

From around 1981 there began a differentiation on the left between those who were dubbed the 'soft left', of which Hain was one, and those who were traditional 'hard left'. There was a great deal of tension in the group. It was probably the fact that Cherie joined the executive of the LCC which started the rumours that she was far to the left of her husband Tony, but Peter Hain remembers that when Cherie came onto the executive after the 1983 election some of the hardline Bennites had left and she was a new moderate replacement: 'There was no formal split but there were some fierce tensions and arguments and some fairly difficult things were said. It was just that we felt that whole Trot agenda was not for us. Cherie came on with a whole lot of new people. There was a ballot of the members and there was also a quota for women and I think she came on the first time it was introduced, as one of the women's quota. She wouldn't have been very well known and I was vice chair at the time and chairing a lot of meetings because the chair never turned up. She had just fought Thanet. After she arrived there was an even more clear split with the hard left. We were moving in a moderate left direction and she was very much signed up for that. I remember her being pregnant. She was very large when she first came on. She was not at all showy, there was no posturing about her, but she was always very clear and quite forceful. She was a very thoughtful member of the executive.

'I think she was on for about three years or so, and her attendances got less frequent. She was certainly more involved than Tony, although Tony came to meetings we held in the Commons. I think she was a person who had pretty strong principles and probably still does. The idea of her being a raving left-winger is wrong. That was not her style.'

The LCC marked the formal end of Cherie's career as a politician in her own right.

She is remembered by all who came into contact with her during her active political years as a moderate and though she may be to the left of Tony Blair, hardly surprising given their different backgrounds, later rumours of her being a firebrand socialist seem ill-founded.

Euan Blair was born on 19 January 1984. The next day a photo of him with his proud parents appeared in the *Darlington Echo*.

> Having an MP for a father is not the only claim to fame for baby Euan Anthony Blair, he's also the grandson of a top show business couple. The 5 pound 12 ounce baby, born in a public ward of St Bartholomew's Hospital, is the son of Sedgefield MP Tony Blair. His wife Cherie is the daughter of actor Tony Booth who recently announced his engagement to Pat Phoenix who starred in *Coronation Street* as Elsie Tanner.
>
> 'Both mother and baby are doing well,' said Mr Blair yesterday. 'We are absolutely delighted. I can hardly believe it,' he added.

Tony Blair must have wondered how long it would be before he would be mentioned in his local paper in his own right as MP. So far his newsworthiness was solidly based on who his father-in-law was.

With a new baby coming the Blairs were hard at work house-hunting in Sedgefield. Peter Brooks, one of the lads who was there at that original meeting that first night, said that he was after a house in Trimdon Colliery but he couldn't afford it so he told Tony about it. Blair came down and had a look at it and he took over the negotiations from Peter. It was a real team effort getting the house.

The Blairs paid £30,000 for Myrobella, a double-fronted brick-built house in Trimdon Colliery, several miles to the north of Sedgefield itself. Sylvia Littlejohns, who worked for Tony as his secretary, remembers their joy when they bought Myrobella, which was, they told her, a big house with genuine Victorian fireplaces. There was a great deal of discussion about what to do with the garden and how to keep it tidy. In the end Tony decided that they would have to hire a gardener but he was very worried about what his constituents would think of an MP who employed a gardener rather than doing the job himself.

Sedgefield is attractive, with a village green, a shady tree or two, and a shop selling brand new imitation antique pottery from China. On offer in the 'bargains under a pound' bin is a second hand honeypot, slightly chipped, with 'A present from Sedgefield' painted on the rim. Around the village green there are some pleasant houses, a three-star hotel and the church of St John Fisher where all the Blair babies have been christened. The small church is closed, with a notice to explain that Father Caden can be found in the presbytery in the street behind.

On the road out to Trimdon there is a new-looking restaurant called Ministers. It is the only restaurant in the village. Until 1999 this was a curtain shop but a local couple decided the village needed a restaurant now that it had a Prime Minister. The Blairs hired Ministers and entertained ninety guests there for the christening of their fourth child Leo in May 2000.

Trimdon Colliery has none of the charm of Sedgefield. The miners' houses are mean 1960s terraces with quite a bit of pebble-dashing. There's no mine now, so Trimdon Colliery is a greenfield site with a few scattered shops. The 'local' paper comes from Hartlepool, eight miles down the road.

The green fields look pretty enough when we see the Blairs striding across them at election time, but Myrobella is very close to the housing behind it and it's hard to see what the Blairs did to entertain themselves every weekend for ten long years before Tony became leader of the Labour Party, the kids got older, and they all stayed more often in London.

I wonder how Cherie stood it every weekend. Did she wander up through the village in the afternoon for a copy of the Hartlepool paper? Did she get friendly with the women in the houses behind and pop round for a cuppa? Somehow it didn't seem likely. And then I remembered what I used to do on gloomy Saturday afternoons in Grimsby after a hard week's work in London. Sleep.

John Burton told me that once the Blairs had got their house they were always bringing friends up from London: 'We have had some very interesting people here. We had some good times. Especially New Year. I remember one time we all played games because Cherie was keen on quizzes. I think John Lloyd, the journalist from the *New Statesman,* was on my team and Barry Cox was on another team, but of course you can't compete with Cherie. She always wins.

'We used to have a cricket team at school for staff. Tony had a couple of games for us and we invited him and Cherie along to the annual do. We decided to have a quiz and we split up into teams which was quite disastrous because I wasn't on Cherie's team which walked the quiz! She is so good at these things and so bright and so clever of course. She did literally walk away with this quiz. Tony won't join quizzes because he is not as good as Cherie.'

Lily Burton added that Tony's great strength was looking after the kids. 'He always has played his part with the children especially. I think he truly believes that it is the right thing to do. He gets to enjoy his children, getting up through the night with them. It is all part of enjoying your babies as they are growing isn't it. And being close to them. I think he likes to do that and is very much in control of the family side of things.'

John Burton told me the locals joke about it. 'Paul Trippett, who was one of the men who was present when Tony first arrived, said that when he comes back in a second life he wants to come back as Tony's nanny, because Tony gets up during the night and if there are any problems with the children he sorts them out. Cherie looks after them when she is at home, and weekends they are with Tony and Cherie all the time and so he thinks the nanny's job is perfect.'

The Burtons both agreed with others I have spoken to who are close to the family: Cherie's way of managing is in a sense not to manage at all. She lets life go on around her: chaos might develop, the children may be noisy and overexcited, but she just lets things happen and sort themselves out. She remains calm and cheerful at the centre of the storm. John Burton recalls: 'When they were younger this place would be full of children and they would be charging around the garden in and out of the house creating chaos and Cherie just takes all that in her stride. I would be thinking, 'for God's sake let's have some peace', but Cherie just lets it happen. I'm thinking, 'Oh get them out of here, kick their backsides and let's have a bit of peace', but oh no: she would just accept it. She never seems to trouble at all.'

For years the Blairs went to the constituency almost every weekend. It is three hours by train. Sometimes they drove up. I asked John Burton to tell me about Cherie's legendary driving. He roared with laughter and said I shouldn't be asking. 'The local garage man has rebuilt most of the car that Cherie first came up in, I think. She just gets in the car. Whoop, there you go! There were no worries at all. She was quite cavalier about it. They'd sail off to the town. Her and the kids. She takes everything in her stride. Off to the pantomime at Christmas and everybody has to be included.

'When Cherie had Nicky, Tony got a telephone call that she had been rushed into hospital. He was up here and she was down in London. He was visiting the constituency and he didn't have a car, he didn't have anything and he wanted to see the baby born. He jumped in my car and shot off to London about midnight. He drove through the night. Sadly he didn't make it in time and about a fortnight later I was asking 'Where is my car, can I have my car back please?''

The Blairs had a close circle of friends and managed to have a normal family life. No one turned and stared at them in the supermarket or the street. They were saved from the tensions which build up for families who live all the time in the constituency and feel they are constantly being watched.

Cherie and Tony shared more than most. They had started out on an equal footing, both barristers who wanted to become MPs, and they went on sharing responsibilities for everything once the children arrived. Tony would often go home from the House of Commons and have tea with the children while Cherie was still hard at work in her chambers. Cherie was of course the major wage earner. In the mid-1980s Members of Parliament were paid less than £20,000 a year and had very little money for staff and office costs.

When the Blairs went on holiday abroad Cherie would foot the bill. A friend of the time reported: 'We went on holiday with them once, a whole group of us to Tuscany. We took a villa. At that time they had two or three kids, and a nanny. They were by far the biggest group. Only one other couple had a child. Nannies were very much part of the Blairs' lives in those days. They always had someone living in, they couldn't manage without. By then Tony Blair was a Treasury spokesman when Roy Hattersley was Shadow Chancellor. Cherie was the mother now. Their relationship was much more fraught because they had young kids. Cherie was serene about them. She would come out to the pool, sit down and read a book and leave it up to the nanny. If they howled, which they did all the bloody time – they were really noisy kids – she would occasionally tell the nanny to look after them. Tony would constantly say, "Cherie, Cherie, why don't you do something about those kids?" They were always rowing but it was contained. It was about a young married couple with young kids, neither of whom wanted to be overburdened. She was clearly not going to be a wonderful nurturing mother, she wanted a rest. After all she was a barrister as well. He wanted a rest. He had brought a book with him which was *The History of Europe*, one of those thick Penguins, something like eight hundred pages and it was about a third read when he came and about a third read when he left.

'It was very pleasant: there was a nice pool and we went on nice walks and had nice dinners and stuff. There were long walks, with Tony and the others talking about what to do about the Labour Party. Occasionally we would all join in, and round the dinner table in the evening we would talk about it, but not so often. After all, there were other things to talk about. Cherie would often say, "Oh for goodness sake leave it alone!", but by that time it was clear Tony was one of the up-and-coming stars, and he was always saying, "What do you think about this? Suppose we did that?" Constant questions, testing out scenarios.

Cherie would be brusque and dismissive of it, not dismissive of the conversation but I don't remember her entering into it then.'

Another friend remembers that Cherie even then was absolutely clear about her priorities. She wanted time and space for herself. She was certainly never in awe of Tony's job and she expected him to take equal shares in all that they did. 'Cherie would lie out on the sunbed in her glasses acquiring a suntan and reading. Lady Muck springs to mind. I on the other hand had this sort of working-class mother sense – you know, the woman does it all – and was slightly horrified, but Cherie didn't have that. She seemed to be saying, "I'm here on holiday, we've got a nanny – fine!" Tony didn't have that.

'Cherie didn't seem to worry about it at all. She was quite happy for Tony to clear up, to sort out the problems while she got on with having her holiday. I couldn't quite understand it then. It was as if she came from a different background altogether.'

Those of us who were mothers at the same time can only look back at Cherie with admiration. At a time when we were all dashing about minding our kids, getting in a bit of work when we could and never making it to the gym or the swimming pool, here was someone who got her priorities right and made sure she had time for herself. Here was someone whose husband cared enough to share the responsibilities for childcare while climbing the political ladder. Ann Cryer and I were talking just after she had become an MP about how our husbands used to behave. They always managed to make us believe that whatever they were trying to achieve was more important than what we were doing. They were 100 per cent successful. Cherie was strong when we were weak. 'She believed in herself,' as her teacher Norah O'Shaughnessy had pointed out all those years ago at St Edmund's primary school. 'She thought well of herself, she never had any doubts,' said her sixth-form friend Elizabeth Simpson.

Somehow Cherie seems to have been born with a confidence in her own abilities which certainly eluded many of the rest of us.

Cherie's other advantage was the husband she chose. Tony Blair was a new man before his time. He was a modernizer in the Labour Party and he was a modernizer at home. At a time when most of his colleagues were still taking shameless advantage of their women, expecting them to go out and work full time and take all the responsibilities at home, Tony Blair was prepared to go 50–50 with Cherie. Other couples, where almost all domestic duties and child care duties were done by the wife, were surprised when they saw the Blair marriage from the inside.

Tony Blair was putting what were still new ideas to work in his marriage, but had also gone to Westminster determined to shake things up. He wanted to use politics as a way to put his ideas and plans across. He and Gordon Brown were the two outstanding newcomers of 1983. They were in a way just as they are today, Blair full of charm and persuasive about his ideas, Brown diligent and prudent and getting the hard work done.

Sylvia Littlejohns had a part-time job as Tony Blair's secretary when he was first elected. She says she knew straight away that she was working for a man who was going places. 'You could tell,' she said. 'He had ideas of his own and he was confident about them.' She also remembers that he was constantly criticizing the Labour Party and planning ways to change it.

Nowadays MPs tend to have small suites of rooms and either share with their secretaries and research assistants or have them right next door. In the 1980s workers could be miles from their bosses and very few shared offices with them. Sylvia worked in the old Norman Shaw North Building, sharing with Peter Shore's secretary and Michael Foot's secretary. Tony Blair had a desk in a corner of the Cloisters under the main Palace of

Westminster building. He shared the tiny space with the extreme left-winger Dave Nellist when he first arrived, but soon Nellist was replaced by Gordon Brown. If Tony wanted to talk to Sylvia he went over to the Norman Shaw building and sat on the edge of her desk. Tony and Sylvia hadn't been together very long when Anji Hunter turned up as a researcher. Sylvia, on the lookout for a full time job, asked Tony if she could be his researcher when she found out Anji was coming, but he said no. Accommodation was so scarce that Anji and Tony shared a desk for quite some time.

Sylvia remembers that Tony talked about Cherie a great deal. 'I knew she was clever because he was always saying so. Tony had a great deal of admiration for Cherie's cleverness.' Sometimes Cherie would come in to the House with the two children for tea on the terrace, and Sylvia met her then. Sylvia thought she was very nice and quite like all the other young wives with small children who were around in those days. Sylvia's summary of the Blairs is that they were very young and very happy and very pleased with each other.

Cherie's involvement with the party through the later Kinnock years was solely as a spouse. During the 1987 General Election she stayed in London and went to work during the week, then transported the kids to Sedgefield at the weekend. Like every MP, Tony Blair put his wife and kids on show at election time. Euan had been joined by a baby brother when Blair's second son Nicky was born in December 1985, and after the 1987 election Tony bounced joyfully into Sylvia Littlejohn's office and told her that he and Cherie had managed to conceive another baby during the campaign. Love and politics seemed so intertwined for the MP for Sedgefield and his wife that it was hard to separate them.

Kathryn Hazel Blair, named after Cherie's cousin and Tony's mother, was born on 2 March 1988. A few days after giving birth Cherie was back at work, arguing with Fredric Reynold amiably enough about a woman's right to maternity leave. Reynold seemed to have the idea that if you'd had one baby the rest would be plain sailing, but Cherie corrected him.

There was an extra dimension to women's work in the 1970s. In very many cases not only was a woman a worker, a mother and a wife; she had to look at all times as if she didn't have any children to care for, and was expected to make up for time lost in things men didn't have to do, like attending ante-natal classes and having babies.

Frederic Reynold explains: 'Just before she gave birth to Kathryn her third child she was my junior in a sort of test case brought by a shop steward at Heathrow against British Airways. It concerned the right to contractual bonuses. Cherie did manage to juggle attendances at the ante-natal clinic with dutiful appearances sitting behind me. I missed her occasional absences but she persuaded me it was important. I remember taking less than a chivalrous and sympathetic view at the time, for which I was sternly rebuked, but she compensated by working with me in Chambers on the occasional Sunday and again she was extremely helpful. She combined her role then as a mother, and expectant mother with working for me expertly.

'She was warm, generous, always happy to be teased, and she was teased quite often. That artlessness was one of her most endearing qualities. She would be enormously enthusiastic, loyal and affectionate, and I regarded her as a very good friend over the years. There was never any side to her and if she disagreed strongly about anything she disagreed strongly. She didn't resort to dissembling euphemisms. You knew exactly where you stood and I rather liked her forthrightness.

Although sensitive souls might have regarded her occasionally as verging on the tactless I found it on the contrary a breath of fresh air.'

Nine

WIFELY AMBITIONS

In the early 1990s, just after John Smith became the leader of the party, the editor of the *Sunday Times* Andrew Neil sent the journalist Barbara Amiel to spend the weekend with the Blairs at Myrobella. The resulting article, entitled with amazing presience 'Labour's Leader in Waiting', explained that Blair was hoping to build a new kind of Labour Party and dealt mainly with his big ideas for the future. But it also gave an intriguing insight into Cherie as she was then.

When Amiel arrived in Trimdon Colliery late on Friday afternoon Blair was already in the constituency with the children. Blair and Amiel set off by taxi in the early evening for Blair to take part in *Any Questions?* just down the road in Stockton-on-Tees. The taxi driver, turning left onto the dual carriageway at Sedgefield, ran straight into the side of a lorry. There was glass and metal everywhere, but no one was hurt. Tony Blair was stood in the middle of the road carefully picking up shards of glass. Just at that moment a battered car came round the corner, driven by Cherie Booth.

Later in the weekend Amiel tried to interview Booth about her husband and found her shy and difficult:

> Cherie does not revel in being the political wife. She tries very hard but easy chat does not come naturally to her. 'I occasionally buy things for him,' she says of her husband, but doing the routine political wife interview is like pulling teeth. Ask her about Tony's habits or attitudes and her face closes, the eyes rebuke you and she becomes monosyllabic. 'Actually, he rather enjoys buying his own clothes,' she will tell you if pushed. The sentences come out rat-a-

tat-tat. 'I encourage him. He plays tennis, doesn't go to an exercise class, likes walking, has very general tastes in music. Is there anything else you'd like to know?'

Amiel quotes another Labour MP, who had found Cherie 'charmless and difficult'. However, despite her lack of welcome, Amiel had a grudging respect for Cherie, who will not be patronized as the Member's Wife:

> To her undying credit, Mrs Blair refused to pretend that I was welcome. She responded in monosyllables to my slightly gushing attempts to make conversation. Her politics insofar as she expressed them at a dinner made somewhat difficult by her stony silences and her husband's compulsive filling in, seem marginally right of Mrs Mao. I got the distinct impression that while I would be included in Ms Booth's embrace of mandatory quotas for females who deserved to go places in the judiciary, my destination was more likely to be the cells than the bench.

I laugh at all this and sympathize absolutely with Cherie. How many times in Grimsby struggling to look after the kids and worrying about the work I was going to do next week did I brush off constituents and journalists who asked over and over again, 'What's he really like at home?'

Barbara Amiel begins to realize that Cherie is her own woman:

> The prospect of her husband rising in the Labour Party pleases her but Cherie senses that it could be a problem for her professionally since her work involves her with the local authorities. The truth is that although Cherie would rather submit to the rack than complain, her life is bloody hard work. She is raising three children, commutes to the constituency every weekend, has a husband whose profession keeps him on the dinner circuit more than any family

would want, carries a full load as a barrister and puts a supportive face on Tony earning far less than he might in his original profession of the law.

'Look,' she says, 'Tony is ambitious but he often tells me that politics is not his whole life. If he wanted he could walk away tomorrow. At the end of the day when things are going badly he can see the children and realize that there's something else in life. When it came to the deputy leader's job Euan said he was glad his Daddy had chosen to spend more time at home. I think Tony is incredibly talented and I want him to succeed. He's got an incredible amount to offer but we've got young children and they need to be protected. Life when my father was at the height of his fame had its problems for me. I understand it.'

This is one of the few times that Cherie has drawn attention to how much she suffered as a child because of her father's fame. Cherie must feel that whatever else life brings, if she can save her children the humiliation she suffered as a child, she will have done a good job.

By 1992 Tony was Shadow Home Secretary, and his good looks and his charm meant that he was getting a high profile outside the Westminster village. If Cherie was going to catch up with him it had to be now.

Cherie made the key move to work with her great admirer Michael Beloff QC at his Chambers in Gray's Inn Square. Michael Kaplan, her clerk there, said that Cherie had been interested to get into more public authority and employment work. They'd had loads of it on offer and she came along at the right time. Cherie began to develop her profile as a barrister as Tony got nearer to the top in the Labour Party. By now people had begun to see Blair as a potential leader. Michael Kaplan said that as Blair's fame grew working with Cherie had become more difficult. A lot of people started wanting to instruct her because of who she was married to, and a lot of other people stopped wanting to instruct her because of who she was married to. Kaplan says that in the end he thought she lost more work than she gained, but they were climbing together and people began to talk of Cherie as a top barrister destined to become a Queen's Counsel at the same time as they talked of Tony Blair as Britain's next Labour Prime Minister. The myth of the golden couple was born.

Cherie had found herself well suited to fight the behind-the-scenes battles to support her husband and make sure he won the Labour leadership. Winning arguments by intellectual prowess was what she did successfully at work every day of the week. She took a case, studied it carefully, and worked out how to come out on top. She proved adept at doing the same thing for her husband.

Many people have suggested that Blair and Booth had a pact about their futures. Did Tony and Cherie agree that the one who was first chosen for a safe seat would go ahead and get to the top in politics while the other one did law and made the money? It's highly unlikely. If Cherie had got to Westminster first there's no way that Blair would have accepted it as the end of his political career. He was upset and fed up in 1983 when it seemed that his only role in the General Election would be as the Candidate's Spouse. At absolutely the last minute he discovered that highly winnable Sedgefield needed a candidate, and he managed to engineer himself onto the shortlist. Tony Blair seems to have made his mind up that he wanted to be a politician first and foremost from the day he joined the Labour Party. He saw politics as the way of achieving his goals for a better society and he wasn't about to be diverted from that. Like most women Cherie was much more flexible. She wanted to be an MP, she wanted to be a barrister, but she knew that as a woman she had to take other things into consideration. She was a wife who was very much in love with her husband, she was a mother of a growing band of small children and she had strong ideas about how she wanted to bring them up. Most people have some plans for their lives and careers but end up adjusting to what fortune brings. It was just the same for Cherie.

During the tough years of producing children as well as going to work Cherie must have realized that law was the easier, more comfortable and practical solution for her. If she had continued to look for a seat and both of them had been MPs the situation would have been pretty well unworkable. Both had strong feelings that their family had to come first and they could never have managed if there were two constituencies to visit as well. Cherie pushed her political ambitions to one side and concentrated on the law as the practical alternative. But that didn't mean she'd waved her magic wand and turned overnight into a housewife.

Cherie has always been ambitious but she has also always been strongly committed to equality in her marriage. She was prepared to give Tony total support in his bid for the top. She also made it clear she would expect the same sort of support from him sometime in the future when she was ready to ascend to the summit. Friends report that she talked often about her plans for her own future and Tony was aware that one day he would be expected to take more family responsibility, but one of the keys to the Blair's relationship is that Tony seems to have accepted from the beginning that equality in everything was his deal with Cherie. Equality was not something that came later to the Blairs because social mores changed. They'd agreed it from the start. Tony had watched Cherie demonstrate her single-mindedness about her career over and over again. There was no pact but there seemed to be an implicit bargain within their marriage.

Both Blairs had believed almost from the moment Tony became an MP that it was likely that he would go a long way in the Labour Party. A growing number of other people had begun to believe that someday Tony would get to the top. The Blairs had talked privately about what they would do when that day arrived. The first public mention came from Andrew Neil, the man who sent Barbara Amiel to interview Blair in his constituency just before Smith was elected leader.

When John Smith died in May 1994, Cherie was as shocked and horrified as everyone else, but she realized immediately that this was something which was going to affect her very much indeed. Smith's death was announced before ten o'clock in the morning and by lunch time Cherie was wondering what Tony's reaction would be. She believed her husband must seize his opportunity now it had come up.

The Blairs' sense of timing had always been impeccable, unlike the Goulds'. Bryan Gould had stood against Smith for the leadership against the advice of just about everybody. Neil Kinnock told Gould that 'Smithy will never last the distance'. Gould couldn't see it and lost disastrously. It was the beginning of the end of his career as a politician. He sat alone in stunned silence surrounded by packing cases in his Cotswolds cottage when he heard the news of Smith's death. He had recently resigned his seat and was packing to go to home to New Zealand to take up a job as Vice Chancellor of Waikato University.

When Tony Blair heard the news he was in Aberdeen campaigning for the Euro-elections. Cherie was at her chambers in Gray's Inn Square. Blair flew back to London alone in the early afternoon and Cherie decided to meet him at Heathrow. She wanted to tell him immediately that she believed he must contest the leadership. She was on her way when she ran into Barry Cox, the TV executive who'd been their next door neighbour in Mapledene Road and was still one of their closest friends. Cherie asked Barry if he would help her to persuade Tony to run, if persuasion turned out to be necessary. Cherie knew that her husband would be hesitant to stand against his old friend Gordon Brown. Cox agreed to give whatever support he could. In fact he became Blair's financial backer and the only member of the leadership campaign team other than Cherie who wasn't working at Westminster.

Blair and Gordon Brown had been close friends since they had entered Parliament. They were shadow Home Secretary and Shadow Chancellor respectively. They were both in their different ways committed to modernizing the party. Now one of them would have to stand down and support the other, if either was to be the next leader.

Cherie's way of operating is different from Tony's. She is tougher than her husband and more direct. She assesses intellectually what needs to be done to achieve a certain aim and she does it. Tony is much more conventional. He's polite and seemingly hesitant. He hovers round a topic listening to what everyone else thinks should happen, waits for people to encourage him to take the course he has chosen. He allows people to persuade him. He's extremely cautious, he doesn't come to basic decisions quickly. They have to grow, not be forced on him.

Opinion polls in the party showed that Blair was the popular choice for leader, yet he remained polite and laid back as ever, keen to do the decent thing right up until the famous 'last supper' at Granita, an Islington restaurant.

Blair's support team was officially led by Jack Straw and Mo Mowlam. Inside the Labour Party in Parliament MPs wanted to know what part Peter Mandelson was playing. Mowlam reassured them he was nothing to do with Blair's leadership campaign, but the role Mandelson played was crucial. He had deserted Gordon Brown shortly after Smith died and given his support to Blair.

There were many councils of war in the Blairs' Richmond Crescent home and Mandelson and Cherie were present at most of them. Cherie always seems to have got on well with Mandelson, later famously inviting him to spend the night at Chequers with the Blair family after his first sacking from the cabinet.

Alastair Campbell and Fiona Millar, soon to be key figures in Blair's team, were in place as favoured journalists, Campbell at the *Mirror*, Millar at the now defunct *Today* newspaper. But it was Mandelson and Cherie between them who convinced Tony that Gordon Brown would have to stand down, and that Tony's duty was to accept it.

It was at Granita Restaurant on Tuesday 31 May 1994, just nineteen days after the death of John Smith, that Gordon Brown told Tony Blair he would not contest the leadership and that he would support Blair's bid. Blair accepted Brown's sacrifice. Tony rushed home afterwards to share his good news with Cherie and Peter. Gordon Brown went to the Atrium Restaurant in the basement of 4 Millbank to share another dinner with his closest supporters.

There has been talk ever since, always denied by the principals of another pact, this time between Blair and Brown. Did Tony Blair make some sort of deal with Gordon Brown that he would give up the leadership at the end of a second term? He has denied it repeatedly.

In the days leading up to the Granita meeting when Cherie had been attempting to put iron into Tony's soul and make him believe that it was right and proper for Gordon to stand aside, they talked a lot about the leadership which inevitably revolved around the more hazy issue of their future together. Eager as always to get things sorted, she kept suggesting ways of making it easier to come to an agreement with Gordon. Her strategy may have gone something like this: 'Tell Gordon you won't be round for ever as leader of the party. Don't forget you owe it to me if I support you now, to give me my chance to get to the top in a few years time when I am still young enough to enjoy it. You know I want to be a judge but I can't do that if I'm supporting you as the Prime Minister's wife in Downing Street. Just tell Gordon that. In fact I'll tell Gordon that myself the next time I see him. You also have to point out to him that you want to be leader now because you are the only one who can win now. It's happening much sooner than we thought, but you have to take the opportunity now it has arisen, and you are way ahead in the opinion polls.'

And then: for good measure, 'Tell Gordon that I been giving you a hard time if you like, because I have to have my turn, and in a few years, say in the middle of your second term we will change priorities. You will have done what you wanted as leader and it will be my turn to get to the top in the law.'

It's the sort of future planning that wives have been doing with their husbands since Adam and Eve. 'Blame me for losing the garden of Eden if you like, my dear, as long as you make sure we win out in the end and stay together.'

Tony Blair has always denied that he made any sort of pact with Gordon Brown, but Brown's supporters are resolute that there was. Probably there wasn't any formal agreement, yet it's surprising that no one has ever asked him what Cherie did. If Cherie managed to engineer a minute or two alone with Gordon to tell him about the Blair family's plans for the future, or if Tony had mentioned his obligations to Cherie's future career, it would have given Brown something to hope for when he bowed to the inevitable, some clever forward planning by Cherie made Brown hear what he wanted to hear.

There were two solid and important reasons why Brown couldn't win. Tony was much more popular in the party, and Gordon Brown's old mate and arch fixer Peter Mandelson had deserted him for Tony Blair.

Relations between Gordon and Cherie are said to be cool. He didn't like it when she requisitioned the flat at Number 11 Downing Street because it was bigger and more suitable for her large family. She is said to have found his then spin doctor Charlie Whelan lounging in the living quarters at Number 11 just days after the election and said icily, 'What are you doing sitting in my house?' Whelan replied in kind: 'It's the taxpayers' house, not yours.'

Gordon Brown is said to have quickly become fed up with the noisy home life of the Blairs. He sleeps most of the time at the flat in Westminster that he bought when Labour were in opposition. For Gordon Brown, Cherie Booth is a constant reminder of his future. He wants to be Prime Minister more than anything else. His future to some extent is in her hands. Will she persuade Tony that two terms are enough for him? Will she remind her husband that it's time for her to begin her final ascent to the legal summit? Brown's chances depend on the Blairs' timing. If Tony were to stay on after the next election Brown probably couldn't win a leadership race. He'd be too old and seen too much as a figure of the past. In some ways Gordon Brown needs Cherie almost as much as Tony does.

Ten

BECOMING MRS BLAIR

I first remember taking an interest in Cherie Booth just after her husband had become leader of the Labour Party. There was a photograph of Cherie with Pauline Prescott at Brighton Races in 1994. Both wore a fresh red rose on their left breast. There the similarity ended. Pauline Prescott was the perfectly attired racegoer – suit, high-heeled shoes, important hat. She'd probably been with her husband to the Members' Enclosures at Beverley, York and Market Rasen too many times to count. Cherie was wearing a boat necked T-shirt, leggings, pixie boots, the sort of belt more usually seen pulling together a dirndl skirt and a peasant blouse, and a blouson jacket. It was the most extraordinary outfit ever to grace the races and it made the front page of many newspapers. The fashionistas rubbed their hands together with delight as they enjoyed this vision of what they described as 'socialist fashion sense'.

I was fascinated by the picture. It said very clearly that Cherie had no idea about the races, had never been before, and hadn't given the occasion a thought. Someone had told her she'd be out in the open air and she'd imagined a sort of works picnic with a lot of standing about eating chicken drumsticks and watching a few horses gallop by.

Who was this woman who cared so little about the social niceties of the role of leader's wife that she was capable of making the same ghastly mistakes as I made so often myself? I still blush with shame when I see a photograph of the Queen's visit to Grimsby in 1979. I'm wearing a green knitted skirt and top, a green rain hat and the Mayor's Serjeant's gloves. (No one had told me that gloves and hat were essential and I wouldn't have believed them if they had.) But I was only a humble backbencher's wife. Tony Blair was the party leader. What was it with Cherie? Didn't she care? Didn't she know? Why had no one told her?

'She found it very hard to begin with,' said her husband just before the 1997 election. 'They criticized her about what she wore and how she looked. Probably she didn't get the clothes thing right to begin with. But she wasn't supposed to be a fashion model.'

Tony Blair became leader of the Labour Party in July 1994 and Cherie was made a QC in 1995. From that moment on there was a public as well as a private Blair marriage.

These days Cherie is blooming with confidence about her work, her family and her friends. Her clothes and shoes have become more expensive, more exclusive. Her hair is glossy, her makeup is careful. She's had the Russian laser operation to tighten her eye muscles so that she no longer needs to wear glasses even for reading. There has been a steady build-up of gloss and confidence since Tony was elected party leader back in 1994.

But when Cherie first stepped into the spotlight as the Leader's Wife she seemed terrified. She appeared in strange outfits like the Brighton Races pixie boots, and she wore suits with long droopy skirts and flat shoes for more formal occasions. Their first appearances as a couple were disastrous too. She clung to whatever part of him was closest to her and looked like nothing so much as a rabbit in the headlights of a car. She looked terrified and dazzled by it all.

Tony Blair told Lynda Lee-Potter that both of them had been pretty terrified back then: 'In some of the early pictures we look as if we are holding on to one another for dear life which we probably were. It was such a strange thing because we'd been married for fourteen years. We weren't used to people photo-graphing us holding hands.'

With all the attention she was getting Cherie felt naked and exposed. It is easy to see why. Being known as someone's wife gives a modern woman no authority at all. It's not like being a barrister where everyone respects you for your intellectual skills in arguing your case. It's not like being a mum where the kids respect you as the authority figure. Cherie now faced up to the awful fact she'd never accepted before. Wives, especially silent ones, can only be respected for how they look.

Cherie was spotted on the Manchester shuttle from Heathrow on the Saturday before the Labour Party conference in 1994. 'I've never seen anyone who paid so much attention to the safety announcements on a plane. She watched the video intently as if it was the only thing in the world that mattered to her.' This was an example of the way Cherie focuses totally on whatever she's doing, to the exclusion of all else. It makes her look fierce and terrified all at the same time. She had been subjected to heavy criticism not only for her clothes sense but also for her uncom-fortable appearance in public.

Cherie is intelligent and perceptive. It was about this time she began to realize that she had not been a success as the 'spouse', the 'better half' at her husband's side. Newspapers gave her a hard time. While some may have found her appearance at a race-course in pixie boots and leggings appealing – it made her seem human and just like the rest of us – fashion journalists were appalled by her lack of nous. Conventional male Labour voters were apprehensive about the wild eyes, the fixed glares and the pawing of the leader. Cherie Booth had managed to make sex on the campaign trail an issue long before Al and Tipper Gore and that kiss at the Democratic Convention in the most recent US presidential election.

Nine-year-old Cherie Booth (centre) in the St Edmund's School choir.
(*St Edmund's School*)

The Seafield Convent Lower Sixth
Form production of *Murder in the
Cathedral*, 1970: Thomas Becket –
Cherie – lies slain.
(*Crosby Herald*)

Cherie in the Lower Sixth at Seafield Convent, 1970.
(*Mrs Elizabeth Glynn*)

THANET NORTH PARLIAMENTARY ELECTION

THURSDAY, 9th JUNE 1983

VOTE FOR . . .

CHERIE BOOTH
Your Labour Candidate

CHERIE BOOTH is 28 years old and a barrister practising in London. She was born and brought up in Liverpool but moved south in 1972 when she went to the London School of Economics. In 1975 she graduated with first class honours in Law. One year later she came first in the barristers' exams for England and Wales. She now has a busy practice, specialising particularly in employment, family and social welfare law. In addition, Cherie is a Governor of an infant and a comprehensive School; gives up one night in every fortnight to work in an East End legal action centre; is a member of her local Community Relations Council; and helped establish in Hackney a local one-parent family action group.

Cherie has been an active member of the Labour Party for many years, introduced to it by her father, the actor Anthony Booth of "Till Death Us Do Part" fame.

She is married to the barrister Anthony Blair and they live in South Hackney in London.

The 1983 General Election: Labour candidate Tony Blair with his wife
Cherie, father-in-law Tony Booth and Pat Phoenix.
(*Mirror Group Newspapers*)

Cherie and her father at Pat Phoenix's funeral, September 1986.
(*Mirror Group Newspapers*)

2 May 1997
(*Mirror Group Newspapers*)

Cherie Booth on the day she became Queen's Counsel, 25
April 1995. (*Mirror Group Newspapers*)

The Chancellor of Liverpool John Moores University
awards an honorary degree to Cilla Black, July 2000.
(*Mirror Group Newspapers*)

The Blair family *en route* to the polling station, 7 June 2001 – Euan, Nicky, Cherie, Tony and Kathryn.
(*Press Association*)

Cherie and Leo outside 10 Downing Street, Friday 8 June 2001. (*Mirror Group Newspapers*)

Cherie had come to the third great crisis point in her life. The first occurred when she was nine and her parents told the world that they were splitting up. The second crisis in Cherie's life happened when she met Tony Blair and he was chosen to stay on in Derry Irvine's chambers while she, the cleverer of the two and the first to be taken on, was sent out into the world to find a new set of chambers. She learned the hard lesson that there was more to success than just being clever. Tony Blair had charm, was persuasive and most of all he was a man. Together these attributes seemed to count for more than her hard work and cleverness. Cherie took what she had learned on board and she adapted. The third crisis in the life of Cherie Booth came when she realized that she was a public relations flop. If she was on show as the smart lawyer people accused her of being rude and chippy and bossing Tony about. If she tried to act as a normal loving wife it came across as fear and skittishness combined. If she acted as she did at work the journalists said she was tough and nasty and the power behind the throne, if she showed them how much she loved Tony by holding on to him and looking up at him then they said she was a simpering fawn.

When he saw how unhappy she was, Blair suggested it might be better if she and the kids stayed out of the limelight alto-gether, and for a few weeks they tried it. Then Cherie said to Tony 'look you're not protecting us by keeping us out of things. We just don't feel part of what you are doing. I'm going to be with you, not in the political sense but as your wife.'

Enter stage manager Alastair Campbell and his devoted assis-tant Fiona. Campbell persuaded the Blairs that if the role Cherie played was tightly controlled and almost 'rationed' Cherie could become a success as the leader's wife.

Cherie did what she had done before when faced with personal failure. She pulled herself together, focused, and worked out a way to survive. Cherie had always loved acting. It was, after all, the Booth family business. She decided she would turn her public appearances into a role, a part she could play. In future there would be two Cheries. Mrs Cherie Blair would appear in public with her husband, she would make sure she wore the right clothes, and she would be friendly and informal with everyone she met. She would say absolutely nothing. If she had to make small talk and the journalists were far enough away she would chatter openly about her kids and her family.

On the other hand Ms Cherie Booth QC would make it clear that she had nothing whatsoever to do with the government and didn't in any way represent the Prime Minister. She would welcome legal cases where she could fight against the government and demonstrate her independence. In her other life as Tony's wife and mother to her kids she would go on just as she had in the past but she wanted as much privacy for that part of her life as privilege and money and the skills of Alastair Campbell could buy her.

Tony Blair told Lynda Lee-Potter: 'She just decided there is no point in running away from it. I am going to make sure I look the part. It's how she operates when she sets her mind on something. She sorted herself out completely. She said, "I can either hide away in which case people will say I am not supportive or I accept that I am going to be in the spotlight. I can make sure at least that I look like a credit to you." She lost nearly two stones. She started to take more of an interest in clothes than she ever did before. She just got herself psychologically attuned to the fact that life was going to be different.'

In fact what Cherie had done was to hire a coach. Lifestyle and fitness consultant Carole Caplin, who had been a member of the group Shock in the 1980s, was given the job of transforming her. Caplin was working as a fitness instructor in the

Albany gym where she met Cherie and convinced her that she could turn her into a PR success. Caplin arrived at Richmond Crescent and began influencing just about every aspect of Cherie's life, encouraging Cherie to get an expensive haircut, spend more time in the gym and spend some money on suitable clothes. Ronit Zilka was the first beneficiary of Cherie's patronage. She made smart and tidy suits and frocks and in the beginning almost all of Cherie's wardrobe came from her. Zilka got a lot of publicity from her relationship with Cherie and her career flourished. People couldn't believe the change in Cherie. Caplin encouraged Cherie's interest in alternative therapies ayurvedic massages, herbal teas and crystals, and Cherie did as she always did with something new, went the whole hog and embarked on her new role with passionate enthusiasm. Carole Caplin even went with Cherie to the 1994 Party Conference in Blackpool to keep her spirits up. In a smart navy suit with velvet trimmings, glossy hair and shiny lips and shoes, the fashion correspondents agreed she had been successfully transformed.

Cherie Blair looked so good the fashion trade began to invite her to their own events. She attended London Fashion Week in 1996 and saw the work of a new young Ethiopian designer Ronan Keflay and ordered a flattering evening frock and matching shoes in sludge green. During the 1997 election her clothes were simple and successful. She began the campaign in plain black trousers and a black and white striped twinset and she ended it in triumph on the steps of Downing Street on 2 May in a sienna coloured suit with a rather fussy collar. The photograph of the Blairs walking into Downing Street was one of the most symbolic of the decade. Cherie gave the suit which appeared in newspapers across the planet to the Museum of London where it's still on display.

But as if to accentuate the transformation and indeed the

need for it, Cherie's most talked about outfit of the election was the night-dress in which she appeared at the door of 1 Richmond Crescent early on the morning of 2 May. Some flowers were delivered from the staff and pupils of Kathryn's school. Cherie, exhausted when she'd got to bed only a couple of hours earlier, opened the front door in yesterday's makeup, eyes heavily ringed with kohl, hair stiff with 'product' and back-combing. That photo too made the front pages around the world and Cherie was appalled. Her mother Gale reassured her that people would feel warm and sympathetic to her slip-up and except for a few carping remarks about her grey brushed nylon nightie most people were delighted to see such a human face to the new first family.

When Tony Blair became Prime Minister on the second of May 1997 things became even tougher for Cherie. People didn't really believe that she would be able to go on with her career once she was living in Downing Street as the wife of the Prime Minister, but to the contrary her career flourished. Note paper was printed 'From the Office of Cherie Booth QC' and gave the magic address 10 Downing Street SW1A 1AA. But she needed some high-quality advice to pull this off. Enter Fiona Millar, hired to protect and advise Cherie in the way that Alastair Campbell had done for her husband since he was appointed Chief Spokesman in 1997.

Neatly, it just so happened that Fiona Millar was Alastair Campbell's partner and the mother of their three children. She too was bent on developing her career. She'd been a reporter on the old *Today* newspaper and amongst her credits was a 1994 interview with one Cherie Blair, leader's wife in which she made her famous remark: 'I started life as the daughter of someone, now I am the wife of someone and I'll probably end up as the mother of someone.' When *Today* folded Millar took a part-time job on *The House Magazine* writing profiles of Members of Parliament. Her work with Cherie began as a part-time position which she shared with another woman, but soon it became obvious that Cherie was going to generate a great deal of work and Fiona has been at her side full time ever since. Officially, there's no such job. Being the Prime Minister's spouse has no official status like the First Lady in the USA. Fiona works for the Department of Events and Visits and reports to Jonathan Powell in the Downing Street hierarchy.

Cherie's new celebrity status meant that there was enough work for a whole Department of the Prime Minister's Wife, but the wife of the British Prime Minister is expected to be an enthusiastic amateur doing what she can in her spare time. She is not always funded by the state even when she is at her husband's side on official occasions. 'There are more rows in 10 Downing Street about who pays for what, Cherie or the Government, than there are about anything else,' said a civil servant who worked there. The Prime Minister's consort is an ill-defined and quasi-official role. Norma Major performed it by living at home in Huntingdon most of the time and writing a best-selling book about Chequers. Mary Wilson, who can still be seen with her shopping trolley in Westminster's supermarkets, was a poetry-writing housewife.

Fiona Millar was transformed into a full-time minder, working opposite her lover Alastair in the day, going home with him to their children in north London in the evening. They provided a neat circle of protection for the Blairs. Requests to one of them would be discussed with the other at home if not in the office. To Cherie's old friends and contacts Fiona Millar has taken on a role similar to Anne Robinson's in *The Weakest Link*. Father John Caden, the Blair's seventy-six-year-old parish priest in Sedgefield who has baptized all four Blair children, says that he doesn't get to talk to the Blairs much any more. He used to be Tony's tennis partner when the Blairs spent most weekends at Sedgefield, and Cherie's confidant. But these days he very rarely gets near either of them. 'I call up and Fiona Millar answers the phone and she always tells me Cherie is in the bath, or Cherie is busy working. I don't know whether Cherie ever gets my messages.'

A lawyer who used to work with Cherie tells the same story. It's OK if she phones the Downing Street flat at the weekends. If Tony answers the phone he will get Cherie to call back if she's busy. A call on a weekday is usually fielded by Fiona: 'Cherie's at a bit of a disadvantage now, if you want to brief her. You have to wait for her to call you back, when Fiona gives her the message.'

Fiona Millar is of course a junior partner in the spin doctor's surgery. She is more awkward and less natural than Campbell who has skills which are acknowledged by everyone at Westminster, whether on his side or not. Campbell does his work and manages to seem friendly and even approachable. Millar seems bossy and a bit frightening. She demonstrated her skills on one journalist during the 2001 General Election campaign. Cherie was having some acupuncture done for a charity in the Midlands. Journalists were asked in for a photo opportunity. Cherie stared straight ahead while pins were carefully inserted in her ear lobes. She turned to a nearby journalist and asked him a question. He started to reply and Millar bustled up. 'Out!', she said succinctly. The journalist protested, Millar insisted, and Cherie was left mouthing her apologies. In her private life Millar is said to be warm, popular and fun. The job of protecting Cherie seems to take a lot of the fun out of her life.

Campbell and Millar take their personal lives seriously like many young couples who got together in the 1980s. They feel that they've made a private commitment to each other and don't need the public endorsement of marriage. The Blairs look like Mr and Mrs Old Fashioned, married and deeply religious, surrounded in government and their offices by 'modern couples' some with partners of the same sex. The moderns tend to be a bit sniffy about the old fashioned romanticism of couples like the Blairs. Harriet Harman, who is also married, has pointed out that for Cherie marriage has always been important and that she was 'immensely proud about it in the days when a lot of us were a bit defensive on the subject.'

No one could deny that Campbell has been a great success in protecting the Blairs. From the beginning he has ruthlessly controlled the images which are projected to the public. Just before Blair became Prime Minister in 1997 there was a meeting of his closest advisers. The names of past close friends and the details of important family events were all listed. Wherever possible schools and universities and people who were close or had been close to the Blairs were warned about future interest and asked to be discreet. Sometimes there was a slip-up. Cherie wrote a paragraph for a charity about the worst time of her life when her mother and father announced that they were going to get a divorce, and how grateful she was to the school teacher who had put her life back on track. *The Times* found Denis Smerdon at home in Crosby and wanted to interview him. Downing Street immediately called him and told him not to talk about his relationship with Cherie. The Blairs must be the first British Prime Ministerial couple who have worked through their pasts and started out with a privacy policy and a loyalty bond in place with old friends and family from their first few days in Downing Street.

Nanny Rosalind Mark was asked to sign a retrospective confidentiality document which covered the years in opposition as well as the present Prime Ministership

James Parle, Professor of Medicine at Birmingham University, was a friend of Cherie's when she was at Seafield and he was at St Mary's. When I called him he said he would be delighted to talk to me about their friendship, but only if Cherie gave her permission. His mother back in Liverpool told me that James is very lucky and often invited to events and great occasions when the Prime Minister and his wife visit the Midlands.

Residents of Richmond Crescent in London N1 say that the Blair's immediate neighbours (the houses are so close together that you can hear next door's alarm clock ring through the partition wall) were invited to the Trooping of the Colour and other state occasions when the Blairs moved from Number 1 Richmond Terrace to Number 10 Downing Street, and there was a general street agreement not to talk to journalists who came round the doors.

The main feature of Cherie's successful 1997 election campaign was not her clothes but her silence. What we know of her, of her successful career and flamboyant family, sat very oddly with the silent role she stuck doggedly to. But this seems to have been her very well thought out strategy which she had been devising in the early 1990s when she revealed in a *New Woman* interview:

> These days I have to be careful about what I do and say. I can't always say what I think because I don't want people assuming that's Tony's opinion too. The better known he becomes, the more important that will be. If I didn't actually believe in what Tony was doing it would be far more difficult to cope. But I'm very proud of him. I think he's got a lot to offer and I really want him to succeed.

She stuck absolutely to her plan that her Mrs Blair role was a non-speaking part, and when the Blairs entered Downing Street for the first time most people including me had never heard her voice. It was some months later when the Blairs visited South Africa and Cherie visited a township and spoke to the locals informally that her deep and pleasant voice was heard for the first time on British television.

Cherie was happy that she had begun to combine her two roles so successfully. Members of the public were happy with her. You could see she loved her husband. She was devoted to him and pleasant and helpful at his side. She spent generous amounts of time on charity work and was praised for that too. She appeared frequently enough in high profile cases in the courts for feminists like me to be delighted that she seemed fearless and prepared to stand up against her husband's government if it was in the interests of her client. However, Mrs Blair had not won over all quarters.

Barbara Amiel, who spent a weekend with the Blairs in Sedgefield when Tony was shadow Home Secretary and had been critical of Cherie, decided that she liked the old Cherie better than the usually silent Mrs Blair.

> Curiously, if I didn't like her, I did respect her. There's something very attractive about people who refuse to dissemble. I may have been writing about her husband but sod it, she didn't have to pretend she and I were not at odds. Alas she was doomed. The image makers moved in and Cherie Booth became Mrs Tony Blair. Now on the few occasions we meet, her trapped lupine snarl has evolved into a warm smile and we are simply two girls chatting as we go in to dinner.

Whether or not we like the results of Cherie's strategy, it seems at least until now to have achieved her ends.

The BBC journalist Nicholas Jones believes there is a solid reason why 'Mrs Blair' is a non-speaking part. 'In the last seven years since Blair became party leader, I've heard Cherie Blair speak on two or three occasions. They mainly have been at semi-private occasions, receptions given by trade unions, that sort of thing. She would say a few words, they would mainly be words of welcome or light-hearted remarks, but she's very careful not to stray into politics. And I think this undoubtedly has been a very successful strategy on her part. Because at no point can the media say, and that is what they are very fearful of, that she is the power behind the throne. Cherie never speaks out of turn, because she knows that could be used by the media as a weapon to damage her husband'

The reality, however, is that of course Cherie is a powerful woman with views of her own. She undoubtedly expresses those views forcibly to her husband. The deceit is that those who protect the Blairs feel that they must protect us from this at all costs. Campbell and his team believe that it would be really bad for Tony's image if the true extent of Cherie's closeness to him and the influence she wields were demonstrated publicly. This is one of the reasons why the image of the silent, adoring Cherie Blair, passive at her husband's side, is projected so enthusiastically.

What we have all lost out on is any insight into the private life of Cherie. What Cherie has found is a taste for the privacy that money and power can buy. As Campbell and Millar became more successful in keeping the world at bay, Cherie found that she could enjoy being herself much more inside a protective cordon.

When journalist Anne McElvoy asked Fiona Millar why Cherie wanted it that way, Millar responded snappily:

> Why should she be more public? What's in it for her? She's very happy the way things are. She gets herself to work at Matrix or the court. She goes shopping or to the gym by herself. She has a bit of normality in other words. Why would she kiss goodbye to all that. Why would she do that? You tell me?

Whenever the marriage of Tony Booth and Cherie Blair is being discussed, the same item is always at the top of the agenda. 'Who is the smarter? Who is the cleverer?' Is she brighter than he is? Was it simply chance that he was the first to get a winnable parliamentary seat? Could it have been Prime Minister Booth as easily as Prime Minister Blair? Or was it all, as Bob Dylan sang, a simple twist of fate?

On *Desert Island Discs* Sue Lawley put the difficult question to Tony Blair with extreme caution: 'She is allegedly, legally speaking anyway, a whole lot cleverer than you. Is that right?'

Blair replied without hesitation: 'Oh yeah. Absolutely. She's a brilliant lawyer. The first bit of the pupillage, I was struggling a bit. She helped me enormously. We were doing the Bar exams, which I did not treat with the seriousness they deserved. I didn't work particularly hard at it, but I always remember Cherie being in the Lincoln's Inn Library, when everyone else would go down to the pub for lunch. She was eating her sandwiches in there and poring over her books.'

Michael Beloff QC has no doubts either. He confessed: 'I think she is cleverer than he is.' When asked what qualities Tony has that Cherie doesn't, Beloff says that he doesn't know, but that Blair is a late developer. 'I think Cherie is much the more interesting of the two.'

This question of who influences whom is behind the intense scrutiny that anything Cherie says publicly is subjected to. 'Is she telling us what Tony thinks, or is she telling Tony what she wants him to think?'

Eleven

Unto us
a Child is Born

Westminster is a village really. You see the same MPs and Officers of the House in the supermarket every morning, buying the same breakfast supplies. Baroness Betty Boothroyd, until recently Speaker, can be spotted in Sainsbury's with her crimson coat and matching shopping trolley. Some claim to have seen the Blair kids with Cherie in the local video shop.

The Victoria Medical Centre is a shabby but incredibly busy inner city practice just near the mainline station. You ascend some steep stairs. There's a chair-lift for those who can't manage the climb. The stairs open out onto a small waiting room. The receptionist sits opposite the stair head, and makes eye contact with you as soon as you get to the top. The wall decoration consists of pretty much every pamphlet and notice issued by the Department of Health over the last couple of years. The chairs are in rows around the walls and there's the regulation pile of dying magazines, a few books for toddlers and plastic toys. It's impossible to have a private conversation with the receptionist. Whisper, and everyone strains to hear.

No doubt all London doctors are incredibly busy but this one is always crowded for a special reason. If you are a bit on the cuddly side, this is the practice for you, all the doctors are all generously proportioned. They range from the chunky to the seriously podgy. Such a conspicuous display of human frailty in health professionals cheers everyone up. Roy Hattersley, who also comes here, mentioned in his *Guardian* column how comforting it was to have a GP who was made of more solid stuff than he was. Since Labour got into power in 1997 a couple of quite slim doctors have joined the team but they are outnumbered as well as outweighed.

A signed photograph of Cherie, Tony and Leo on the doctor's desk attests to some even more famous patients. Their GP breaks a bit of confidentiality: 'They are a lovely ordinary family you know. Just like the rest of us. Cherie has been absolutely marvellous with Leo. She's brought him to all our mother and baby classes here and breastfed him with all the other young mothers.' And then she said again as if she couldn't quite believe it herself. 'They're an ordinary family, just like you and me.' It's the most common description people use of the Blairs. Everyone who comes into contact with them stresses how ordinary they are. How normal.

The Blairs may well be normal for a Prime Minister's family, but they are in no way ordinary and the more people who try to convince me of their next door neighbourly qualities, the more extraordinary they seem. The announcement of Cherie Booth's pregnancy with her fourth child in the autumn of 1999 stunned the nation and distracted the population from the government's performance at a time when people had begun to mutter that Blair's long honeymoon with the voters was drawing to a close. Cherie was forty-five, Tony two years her senior. Only 500 babies a year are born to women over forty-five. Naturally the slightly preposterous rumours began that the Blairs had tried for a baby to improve their already solid popularity rating but there seems little doubt that the pregnancy was a happy accident.

American journalist Warren Höge was given the kind of access to the Blairs that British journalists only dream about. His profile of Tony Blair appeared in the *New York Times* magazine in May 2000. In a cosy chat in Tony Blair's Downing Street study he was told the inside story of the announcement which had amazed the nation back in the autumn:

> I was here at the desk writing my party conference speech, and she came to me and said 'I've got some news for you and it's going to be rather shocking about the family'. Well, I immediately thought there was something wrong with our kids. She said there was nothing wrong with the kids we had.'

Höge says Blair laid heavy emphasis on the word 'had' and rolled his eyes. Cherie had then said to him 'But Tony, I think we are going to have another.'

Blair was amazed and says he asked all the obvious and usual questions. Probably the same ones the press came out with when they heard the news. Where? And when? After his wife gave him a bit of detail to support the facts Tony Blair struggled to tell her it was wonderful news, but he says it took a few minutes to pull himself together after the shock. He was coy but a bit wolfish about where conception had taken place. Not Italy, not Balmoral, probably England. He acknowledged there was certainly a choice.

Later Fiona Millar said proudly: 'Let's just say that the fact that they produced a surprise baby when she was forty-five is a testament to a pretty strong and lively relationship.'

When Cherie told Tony her news the Blairs had just come back from the Commonwealth Heads of Government conference in South Africa. Claire, the wife of Don McKinnon, Secretary General of the Commonwealth, remembers chatting with Cherie and Gaynor Cook. Claire, also in her forties, had a toddler son. Cherie asked her enthusiastically, 'Do you think you might have another one when you come to London?', and there followed a bit of a chat about older mothers. Cherie was obviously thinking about the possibilities of a late baby even if she wasn't quite sure yet that she was pregnant.

Fiona Millar accompanied Cherie to her GP for the visit that confirmed her pregnancy, which points to a closeness in their relationship which goes far beyond that of a woman and her press officer. The thought of Fiona Millar sitting quietly in the waiting room of the Victoria Medical Centre while Cherie gets her good news seems hard to believe, but it's rare to see Cherie in public these days without Fiona Millar if Tony Blair isn't present.

I went to watch Cherie in court just four days before Leo's arrival and there in the back row was Fiona Millar in a summer frock and a cardigan with a shopping basket and her purse and a paperback novel to read discreetly during the duller moments.

At a supper meeting for Labour members' wives in an upstairs room above a pub around the corner from Downing Street, Cherie popped in to say hello before dashing off to dine with her husband at home. Fiona followed her around, mobile phone clamped to her head, 'It's Tony for you Cherie', she said at one point and passed over the phone.

'Tony', said Cherie, 'wants to know what time I will be back for my tea' – and she giggled.

Warren Höge was allowed to breach the magic circle surrounding the Blairs and travel with them to Russia when Cherie was seven months pregnant. In their car on the way from the airport into St Petersburg Höge observed that they chatted excitedly like any couple of tourists on a new adventure. Cherie snuggled up to her husband, said she had missed seeing him over the last few days, put her head on his shoulder, worried about whether he had enough clean shirts to last out the trip, and patted her tummy and announced the baby had woken up. Life behind closed doors with the Blairs sounds so perfect that it's hard to relate it to our own imperfect lives where there are never enough clean shirts and husbands in the back of cars are slumped in morose silence.

Höge felt that Cherie's behaviour was genuine and natural, but the Blairs were unlikely to have forgotten that travelling in the car with them was the London Bureau Chief of the *New York Times*.

Charles Falconer, Blair's friend since school days, painted a more realistic picture of Cherie off camera and out of the clutches of Fiona Millar. 'The defining feature about Cherie which has made what is a quite complicated life possible for both of them is the fact that she is so disorganized. She's not managed to be a really successful lawyer, mother of three children and the involved wife of the Leader of the Opposition and now the Prime Minister by great organization. She's done it by just, as it were, accepting.'

Falconer suggests that unlike many women Cherie doesn't panic. She doesn't stare up the mountain at what needs to be done, or make herself dizzy looking down at what she has achieved. Neither does she run her life from inside a hard professional shell. Cherie has often been compared to Hillary Clinton but Lord Falconer disagrees. 'She is shy, diffident. Hillary Clinton is a zillion miles from Cherie; a hard, well organized, politically motivated lawyer who constantly and effortlessly manages career, political agenda, child and possibly husband.'

'Cherie is not well organized in terms of time. They're always unpunctual. She leaves home late in the morning. She constantly runs late, hurrying to try and get home. But she's always very easy. Everyone wants a neighbour who is uncensorious, accepting. People really want to help her. For Cherie people work beyond their required hours. She is utterly trusting and open. She gets by in a practical way in a pressurized life by people being willing to help her.'

For most of her pregnancy with Leo, Cherie Booth continued her life as Falconer described it. She went to her office most days. She attended to a heavy load of charity and state events in the evenings and she spent as much time as she could at home with the older children. She looked cheerful and pretty and sometimes almost serene, which was a big change from her usual nervous demean.

She was becoming noticeably more confident about her public appearances. She had begun to realize what the minders had known for some time. If Cherie stuck to safe topics, her family, her children, the charities she supported, then she was a better performer on the campaign trail that Tony. She got on well with people. They responded to her impulsive hugs and hand holding. Her working-class origins, her wicked laugh and her pleasingly low voice with a hint of a regional accent were a great advantage. Tony, as hard as he tried to stud his sentences with the glottal stops of the London East Ender, had the charming but distant manner of a middle-class vicar visiting his parishioners. He was never quite comfortable, whether it was with a beer in the Sedgefield Social Club or eating fish and chips from a packet with Calderdale MP Chris McCafferty in a Brighouse chippie.

With Cherie by his side Tony could present a totally convincing picture of Man of the People and wife. When they are together the Blairs touch each other constantly. He puts his arm across her shoulder. He grabs her hand. She moves her body into the lee of his. Cherie is his ultimate reassurance when she is at the Prime Minister's side. It's as if she's saying to him. You'll be all right. I know these people I can talk to them, they'll respond to me, and I will be your intermediary. In return you are my defender.

About two months before Leo's appearance Cherie, addressing fellow lawyers at King's College, London on the subject of paid parental leave, gave a big hint that she expected her husband to follow the lead of the Prime Minister of Finland and take paternity leave. Paavo Lipponen had taken officially sanctioned time off after the birth of both his daughters. Finnish fathers are entitled to up to eighteen days after the birth of a child, women are entitled to 105 paid days of maternity leave. In fact Lipponen took just six days leave.

'I for one am promoting the widespread adoption of his fine example,' teased Cherie. Over the next couple of weeks every journalist who got to speak to the Prime Minister asked whether he intended to take paternity leave.

The Prime Minister was in a dilemma. His wife had cleverly turned the Government's rather half-hearted policy on paternity leave into a political issue. First he told John Humphrys on the *Today* programme: 'To be completely honest I haven't thought about it properly yet. I know I should have and I am sure I will. I will decide in the next few weeks. I know I have got to decide soon.'

Blair continued to dither and explained to persistent journalists over and over again that he had a country to run (for country read 'world power' rather than 'small Scandinavian democracy') and he couldn't just down tools and leave things to others. He constantly mentioned the troubles in Sierra Leone where British troops were deployed, and the turmoil in Northern Ireland.

Many female MPs backed Cherie. Harriet Harman, the ex-cabinet minister and old friend of the Blairs, said: 'He is not unique as a Prime Minister but he is unique as the father of that baby.'

Fiona MacTaggart, the Slough MP and a supporter of family friendly workplace reforms, said: 'Of course he has got to take some leave and I think he will but I suspect he will do it in a sheepish way. But we must not be mean to him. All the men are grumbling "it's all right for him" or calling him a dosser. Women are saying, "Do it, do it" and Cherie is giving him big grief.'

As the time of delivery grew near Cherie was photographed constantly going about her work, attending parties, receptions and State events. She didn't look at all tired. She blossomed.

It was ironic that she was working hard on a court case representing the Trades Unions against the Government about paid parental leave. On Tuesday 4 May, just over three days before Leo's arrival, she was presenting her case in the High Court to the soon to be Lord Chief Justice Woolf. It was a hot day for May and when Cherie arrived early with her team she was wearing a thin black cotton frock and clutching a bottle of mineral water. She looked cool and cheerful. She chatted and joked with her colleagues, she read through her notes. Just before the Judge arrived an usher said quietly that if she found difficulty standing for her presentation she could ask the judge for permission to sit down. She nodded and smiled. The other side, the government's representatives turned up just seconds before they needed to be there and seemed a much more formal bunch altogether.

For three hours Cherie Booth stood and spoke. She didn't look stressed or strained but efficient. She did not fiddle or fidget or move her weight from one foot to the other. She didn't even sigh with relief when three hours after she had begun she sat down to listen to the other side. There was a tiny joke about whether and when she would be available to return to court for the summing up. She hoped Lord Woolf would forgive her if she wasn't present. He nodded graciously, she bowed her head in respect. I was seriously impressed. The next day the papers all had photos of Cherie clutching her water bottle and waving at the end of what seemed to me a tough day.

On Friday morning Cherie felt her first contractions. Just after 11 a.m. she was taken to the Chelsea and Westminster hospital in West London in the first family's grey Chrysler people carrier. She was accompanied by the ubiquitous Fiona Millar. The sex of the coming child was supposedly known only to medical staff, the Blairs had asked not to be told, but Campbell and Millar probably knew Cherie was expecting a boy. They would have convinced themselves that it was essential information, something they had to know, if only to stem a tide of pink bonnets and bootees. One plain clothes policeman was discreetly stationed outside Cherie's room in the maternity ward. Fiona shared the long labour with her, only leaving the room when the Prime Minister visited briefly in the afternoon. He then went back to Downing Street for the rest of the working day.

At 8.40 p.m. he was driven to the hospital in a Ford Galaxy followed by a Range Rover. He looked nervous. He joined Cherie and the midwives.

Anne McElvoy in a profile of Cherie for *Talk* magazine says that as the labour reached its climax Millar was stationed outside in the corridor to make sure Cherie could not be overheard making too much noise by other families in adjacent rooms who might be tempted to tell their tales to the newspapers.

Leo George Blair is the first baby to be born to a serving British Prime Minister for 150 years. The last was Bertrand Russell's father Frances Albert Rollo Russell, son of Lord John Russell born on 11 July 1849. Leo arrived at 12.25 a.m. He weighed 6 pounds 12 ounces. One thousand nine hundred and ninety other British babies were born later in the day.

Several weeks before, Lord Winston, the fertility specialist and child birth expert, had let slip that Cherie Booth would apparently be having her baby by Caesarean section. Her third child

Kathryn had been born this way so no one was particularly surprised and 'the leak' had allowed medical correspondents to write long articles about the advantages of not having to huff and puff through a long labour at the age of forty-five.

But Cherie went through ten hours of labour and Leo arrived naturally. While most newspapers cooed and gooed their delight at the event, Thomas Stuttaford, *The Times* Medical Correspondent, who only days before had written a piece explaining why it was essential that Cherie had a Caesarean, tut-tutted his disapproval and emphasized what he saw as the risks for more ordinary patients.

Once again Cherie Booth had demonstrated what an extraordinary woman she is. She was back home at 10 Downing Street with her baby just three hours after he'd been born. The Blairs, like parents everywhere, spent most of the rest of the night marvelling and wondering at their new arrival and phoning friends and relatives to tell them their good news.

The first visitor of the new day was Tony Blair's Chief of Staff Jonathan Powell who arrived clutching the hand of his two-year-old daughter and a bunch of pink rosebuds. Later in the morning Tony Blair appeared at Morning Mass at nearby Westminster Cathedral with his three older children.

President M'Beki, Ehud Barak, President Cardoso of Brazil and Celia Larkin telephoned with their congratulations. The Queen and the Duke of Edinburgh, William and Ffion Hague and the editors and readers of most tabloid newspapers sent flowers. President Putin sent a telegram.

Tony Blair emerged from Number 10 wearing a soft dark blue shirt and jeans. He was clutching a mug of tea with a picture of the three older children on it. He looked tired and un-Prime Ministerial. 'Cherie and the baby are absolutely fine. He is a gorgeous little boy and they are just resting now.' He grinned and fiddled with his mug.

'We'd particularly like to thank all the staff and doctors at the hospital who were absolutely wonderful and fantastic and helped her through it. It was an ordinary birth, a natural birth. It was quite a long labour so Cherie is quite tired now.'

He said it was the first of his children's births that he had witnessed. 'I feel like any father who sees his baby being born. It's very moving and if any of you have been through it, you'll know it. It was quite a long labour and it went on for quite a few hours, but it was quite a struggle in the end for Cherie.'

Then he confirmed what the bookmakers William Hill and the newspapers seemed to know already. The baby was going to be called Leo after his grandfather.

Tony Blair went back inside and welcomed his brother Bill who'd come from north London to inspect the new arrival and Princess Irina Strozzi who flew all the way from Florence to offer her congratulations. Strozzi is one of the Blair's Italian connections who has loaned them holiday accommodation. After an hour at Downing Street she flew straight back to Florence. She was accompanied by her fifteen-year-old daughter. They visited the London Eye as well.

The afternoon was occupied with a three-hour photo shoot. Mary McCartney, daughter of Beatle Paul, arrived with her camera gear. She and Cherie had got to know each other through Breast Cancer Care. Mary's mother Linda had died of breast cancer a year earlier and Cherie had lost her aunt Audrey and a close friend to breast cancer. One photo was to be given free to the press, while all the others had to be paid for by people who wanted to publish them. The considerable profits would go to Breast Cancer Care and another favourite charity of Cherie's, the Sargent Cancer Care for Children.

Cherie, carefully made up, hair immaculate, was photographed wearing a pair of soft grey flannel pyjamas. Tony had changed into a denim shirt and dark blue chinos. The photos were published around the world.

In a touching reminder to us all that Leo George Blair was a new Labour baby, an ordinary product of the British National Health Service, a midwife arrived at Downing Street at ten past four that Sunday afternoon to check out her charges. Mother and baby were doing well.

Cherie Booth issued a statement:

> It is so long since we had our other three children that I had forgotten quite what an ordeal those last few hours of labour can be. The midwives were fantastic and helped us through. Now that Leo is here I am very tired but full of joy.

On the Monday newspapers around the world rejoiced with the Blairs. *La Republica* noted hopefully that 1848, the last year a child had been born to parents at 10 Downing Street, was the year of revolutions that gave birth to a new Europe. *Corriera della Sera* dubbed Leo the fourth child of the third way.

Leo's arrival, and perhaps the fact that he had been present at his birth, seemed to soften Tony Blair and he acquiesced pretty well completely to Cherie's demands that he should take paternity leave. On the Tuesday following Leo's birth the Blair family headed for Chequers and Tony didn't return to work formally until the end of the Whitsun recess on 6 June.

The Speaker and the Leader of the Opposition had both approved Blair's absence. It was a fairly historic event. Traditionally Prime Ministers only miss Question Time if they are on government business abroad but this time he was less than a hundred miles away at Chequers looking after his new son. John Prescott held the fort while Tony Blair held the baby.

When the Blairs returned to Downing Street it marked the

beginning of the worst period of the Prime Minister's first term. While Cherie looked blooming and had snapped back into shape both physically and mentally, Tony had lost his zing. He looked tired and listless. His hair was greyer and thinner. There seemed little doubt that while Cherie concentrated on a speedy recovery Tony Blair really was taking the night watch for his young son's first few months.

Just before the 1997 election Lord Falconer had tried to sum up the Blairs: 'They are unusual people. Against the fashion. Constantly against the tide.'

Watching from Sedgefield, Blair's agent John Burton and his wife Lily were inclined to agree: 'It's been interesting to watch how she has coped with working and the family, but she is so capable. Of course they have a nanny and things but they still do all the work with the children. Leo comes along and you think 'oh dear me'. I said to Tony it will be nice having a teenager when you are in your sixties and he said 'Thanks very much, John, I think it will be all right' but you can see the love for the baby: it hasn't created any trouble at all. Even Euan will pop in to see if he is all right lying in his cot. They are such a nice, normal family. To be a normal family in a situation like that is interesting because of course they are not a normal family. There have never been children like that in there at Downing Street before.

'Cherie just seems as if she lets it all happen around her. You feel that if you should come along in the middle of all that and say 'right we want you to rush along to Trimdon now and open the church bazaar' she would just do it. She is a very special lady. She could be quite strong and tick you off. I think she has ticked one or two of us off in the past if we haven't kept in line and kept Tony out too late. When he was first elected, I think she was always in charge and quite strong. She would say to me 'you should bring him back here earlier than this' if we had a drink or something and ended up really late. Of course Tony is not a late bird anyway. He was probably just doing it for us. She would tick me off and I would take the blame for things. She is a very determined person, very strong.'

It was a good time to remember this.

Twelve

WOMAN AT THE BAR

When Tony became Prime Minister Cherie bought herself valuable space inside the protective cordon provided by Campbell and Millar to develop her career. She knew she had to establish clearly and from the beginning that as a barrister she was her own woman. Yes, she was the Prime Minister's wife but she would willingly take on his Government in the courts because that was her job. Cherie knew that all her cases would be high profile from now on and there must be no questioning her independence or suggestions that she only took cases where she was on the same side as the Government.

One man who was watching carefully for the effects on Cherie when she moved into Number 10 was Michael Beloff QC, the Master of Trinity College, Oxford. He is always at the top of any list of Cherie's supporters. Famously he met her when Lord Irvine chose Tony Blair rather than her as the one to stay on in his chambers at the end of the joint pupillage. Beloff admires intellectual ability above everything, has always enjoyed women and their company. As a student at Oxford in 1964 he moved the motion which allowed women into the Oxford Union. He thought Cherie was wonderful.

He is also, mischievously, always telling people privately that Cherie is much smarter than her husband, and could easily have been Prime Minister herself.

These days he admires her for how well she is coping with being the Prime Minister's wife as well as doing her work and bringing up her kids. 'She has integrated her working life with her home life so well. The thing is that she's a very able, intelligent and attractive woman.' Beloff says Cherie is bound to get into trouble and attract a lot of attention whatever cases she takes. 'If she takes a right-wing client they will ask why she is trying to put this person who won't pay poll tax into prison. If she takes a left-wing client she'll be asked what's she's doing putting her politics first?'

Officially Cherie has little choice in which cases she takes. The cab rank principle where barristers jump aboard the next case which comes along is a part of the Bar Council's rules. 'A barrister who supplies advocacy services must not withhold those services on the grounds that the nature of the case is objectionable to him or any member of the public or on the ground that the conduct, opinion and belief of the prospective client are unacceptable to him or any section of the public.' So it is very much a condition of Cherie Booth's employment as a barrister that she must defend her clients to the best of her ability however much she might disagree with them.

Cherie's first high-profile case after the election was to act on behalf of a female railway worker Lisa Grant whose lesbian partner Jill Percy had been refused travel concessions by South West Trains. Concessions would have been available to a heterosexual partner, married or not. Booth argued that discriminating on the grounds of sexuality was as unlawful as gender discrimination. The Human Rights Act was not yet in force. The case was lost.

At the beginning of the 2001 Parliament six months after the introduction into English Law of the Human Rights Act it was announced, and there was little public interest and certainly no outcry, that the House of Commons had agreed to give spouse travel passes to the male partner of Ben Bradshaw, the Labour MP for Exeter.

As if to demonstrate the cab rank principle, as soon as the Human Rights Act became law Cherie Booth found herself on the other side of the argument representing Shirley Pearce who had been persecuted by her pupils at Mayfield secondary school in Portsmouth. Shirley Pearce is a lesbian and she'd been taunted by her pupils – had cat food thrown on her coat accompanied by shouts of 'pussy' and worse. The school took no steps to protect her or discipline those responsible. Life at work became intolerable and she was forced to go to the headmaster for help. His response was to tell her to grit her teeth or run away. When the chairman of the governors wrote to her to say that she must have realized that she risked abuse, Pearce went to an industrial tribunal claiming sexual discrimination. The claim was rejected on the grounds that she was discriminated against because of her sexuality not her gender. She appealed and Hampshire Education Authority hired Cherie Booth to oppose it. Booth claimed that the tribunal judgement was correct because neither the sex discrimination legislation nor the Human Rights Act had been drafted to accommodate this particular anomaly.

'It is the government to blame and not my client,' said Cherie Booth determinedly. 'The sex discrimination act is not capable of legislating on matters of sexual orientation. What have the public authorities done to infringe the claimant's human rights? We say nothing at all.' The case lasted for three days and there were no conclusive results. The judges resorted to saying that there were lots of other cases in the pipeline. But it did demonstrate that Cherie Booth QC was prepared to take on either side in any argument, and point her finger at her husband's government when she felt they deserved it.

Cherie certainly managed to convince one of her clients that in her determination to prove herself independent and advance her career she was willing to take on Tony Blair's government.

Stuart Neame, Managing Director of the Kentish brewers Shepherd Neame, believes that Cherie enjoys any opportunity to take on the Government. He says she wants to demonstrate publicly just how independent she is. His company's case against the Government was an application for leave to appeal against the Chancellor's decision to increase excise duty on beer. The whole brewing industry was outraged that duty levels were so much higher in the UK than on the continent, causing the great cross-Channel beer trek and cutting the profits of British brewers.

'We started off with Michael Beloff, and we lost our round in the High Court, so we went to the Court of Appeal. Our written application was refused but we were given a date ten days hence when we could make an oral application. Beloff was going to be in the States so we asked the Chambers who else they could offer and back came the answer: Cherie Booth. Our solicitor said she probably won't appeal to you because of her connections with the government and he assumed that she wouldn't like the case for the same reason. But he was wrong. This was the first decision of Tony's government to be challenged by Cherie. She wanted to do it, and I think she wanted to do it to demonstrate that she was still in the market as an independent barrister, and challenging the government is part of her job. Actually I think she relished the case.

'We had a conference the previous Friday at her chambers. She took ten minutes summarizing where the case had got to. She seemed to have an absolute grasp in a very short time. She had an ability to cut through the complexities and see the root of the problem. Whereas Beloff had tried to spin a web connecting the different points of the argument, Booth focused directly on the possibilities and the problems.

'We met the next Monday, I had told the press that she was going to appear on cheaper beer duty and there were twenty reporters outside the court including Boris Johnson. Cherie said: "Hands up all those who think beer's too dear?" She was totally unfazed. She was very casual and didn't hide away. She hung around with the rest of us and didn't stand on ceremony.

Cherie won the right to appeal.

'Cherie was great. She said, "I'm not going to say goodbye now in private, with a whole lot of photographers waiting out the front." She walked with me through the Public Entrance. It was wonderfully helpful.

'No doubt she does the best for her clients whoever they are, but she was also using the case to show that she is an intrepid barrister, very keen to take on the government. It was an opportunity to make the point publicly and she wanted to do that.'

When the new century began both Tony Blair and Cherie Booth had reached a pinnacle in their careers and in their life together. Tony was the most popular Prime Minister since the war. His government was still way ahead in the opinion polls. Cherie had gained confidence in her role as the Prime Ministerial partner. She was planning to start new Chambers with a group of colleagues, and she was pregnant with Leo, one of only five hundred women in the UK over forty-five who would have a baby in the year 2000. She had always been influential in Bar politics and glowing with her new-found confidence she had begun campaigning again for better conditions for poor students who wanted to follow in her footsteps.

'Do you realize Tony, that I wouldn't be able to afford to become a barrister these days?,' Cherie Booth said to her husband at a dinner with old friends. 'You've got to do something about the amount it costs young people to train to become lawyers today.'

She said it again publicly at the conference of the American Bar Association in London in July when Leo was just six weeks old. 'Women, students, and ethnic minorities deserve a much better deal if they are going to be successful barristers and lawyers. There is a real need for this to happen so that the professions more fairly represent the society they serve.'

Cherie makes few public speeches and most of those are about the legal profession and how she would like to see it modernized and improved. But because she speaks so infrequently everything she says is put under a microscope by journalists, commentators and politicians to see if it will reveal the degree of influence she has over the Prime Minister.

As always, her speech to the American Bar Association contained a moderate and well thought out plea for improvements. First, she reassured her audience – she wasn't in favour of positive discrimination. 'I don't think there is any point in having tokenism and appointing people to a job they cannot do.' She also said that she thought there was a very blinkered view in the profession of the sort of people who should be appointed judges. 'It is essential that judges should represent society as a whole. If judges are seen to be mainly men then there is a danger of alienating the public.' Then she added in case even this seemed immoderate, that a taunt of positive discrimination was always the first refuge of those who were against change. She wanted to see direct discrimination stopped, and indirect discrimination too. There were a lot of false ideas about the qualities necessary to make good judges: 'What we have to do is find criteria for the jobs we are doing that are not based on assumptions of what a real lawyer looks like – that boils down to a white middle-class male.'

In a reference back to her own early career, Cherie told the Bar Association, just as she told her husband, that it was a scandal that anyone with real talent should be denied access to the profession because the cost of qualifying for it was too great.

There was a danger that the practice of law would once again be open only to the privileged few so that working-class students of whom she had been one would not even be able to put their toe over the threshold of the gates of opportunity.

This time Cherie was not pleading a case in a courtroom so she was careful to exonerate her husband's government from blame. She said she knew that the State could not be expected to fund the training of young lawyers. She explained that the government believed that it was not considered reasonable to support those expected to earn large sums of money in the future. 'It was,' she said 'up to the legal profession to do something about it, at the same time guarding against insidious indirect discrimination over the award of scholarships to law students.'

All of this probably would have passed without comment in the papers if the top barrister giving the speech wasn't just Cherie Booth QC but also Mrs Cherie Blair, wife of the Prime Minister. Some journalists seized on Cherie's speech as an indication that the government might favour politically correct positive discrimination. In the *Spectator* Melanie Phillips suggested that Cherie was the force pushing her husband and his team in that direction. The *Spectator* cover picture was a cartoon of Cherie in armour riding into battle. Phillips made a tired recitation of conservative beliefs in an attempt to discredit the fairly harmless remarks Cherie had made. According to Phillips women only work because they have to, and would give up work immediately if they could afford to do so.

'For most women nursing a job and a family is incredibly stressful because they want to be in two different places at the same time. Most working women think full time work hurts their children and puts their marriages under strain with the resulting risk of much greater harm to the children from family breakdown.

'For men, by contrast marriage and children are a spur to work even harder. That's an important reason for the pay gap. Women are less likely to get promoted than men. But that is because their employers are necessarily prejudiced. It's because women choose not to put in the long hours required for promotion. This is because they have other higher priorities in life, or because they just recoil from the competitive ethos that drives most men and a few women even higher up the promotional ladder.'

None of this had anything at all to do with Cherie Booth's remarks about the future of her own profession. But it seemed that the minute she opened her mouth, whatever she said would be taken as a sign of what Tony thought or was being pushed into thinking by Cherie. Melanie Phillips' aim seemed to be to discredit the Prime Minister as a moral ditherer who didn't have the guts to put families before same-sex partnerships. All this because his wife had mentioned in her speech that she wanted Parliament to combat discrimination against homosexuals.

A few weeks later a new storm blew up when Cherie wrote an article in the *Daily Telegraph* with her colleague Rabinder Singh to explain the Human Rights Act. This time there was more reason to examine her remarks carefully. The Act was due to become law in October 2000. In anticipation of it, Cherie, Singh and twenty other top QC's and barristers had set up a new chambers, Matrix, which would specialize in human rights work. The article did nothing to help the government except to explain the new legislation, but it did help Cherie to promote her first big business venture. Cherie had played a very active part in Matrix's conception and now she was doing as much as she could to get some publicity for the launch of her new chambers.

On their chic blue and biscuit website Matrix describe themselves as:

A new legal practice set up in anticipation of the complex challenges facing the law in the new century. The lawyers who set up Matrix aim to innovate in the way legal services are delivered and to move beyond traditional divisions – between practitioners and academics, private and public law, and domestic and international law. They are also committed to collaborative ventures that will break down traditional divisions within the legal profession itself.

But outside the world of barristers and lawyers Matrix's main claim to fame is that the Prime Minister's wife is one of their partners. However much Cherie and her colleagues might protest that she is just an 'ordinary QC', it must have helped the launch of Matrix enormously to have such a star in their firmament. Matrix lists all its thirty-two barristers equally on its website. There is no Head of Chambers. A committee of barristers make the business decisions and practice managers run the Chambers day to day. Matrix are careful to portray Cherie as just another distinguished QC.

Cherie Booth: called 1976, silk 1995 – Cherie practises in employment and discrimination law acting for applicants and respondents. In her public law practice she advises local authorities and other public bodies, and individuals and companies. She lectures widely on human rights and advises on the implications of the Human Rights Act. She has appeared in the ECJ and in Commonwealth jurisdictions, and has sat as an international arbitrator. She sits as a Recorder in the County Court and Crown Court and is a Bencher of Lincoln's Inn.

And then, just in case you haven't quite made up your mind that Cherie is the woman for you, there's a sort of *Good QCs Guide* with recommendations for Cherie Booth QC from the law journals:

A 'leading silk' in Administrative and Public Law (*Chambers Guide*; *Legal 500*)

A 'leading silk' in education (*Chambers Guide*)

A 'leading silk' in employment law, 'does an excellent job and remains very busy' (*Chambers Guide*)

A 'leading silk' in employment law, a 'heavy hitter for the right kind of case' (*Legal 500*)

The only thing Matrix doesn't say is how much it might cost to hire Cherie to do a little 'heavy hitting' for you.

The article explaining the Human Rights Act appeared in the *Daily Telegraph* on 7 August 2000 and caused a political row. This time it was the Conservative Opposition who tried to get at Blair through his wife. Cherie and Rabinder Singh had begun their article: 'The Human Rights Act forms an integral part of the Government's programme of constitutional reform, which has the aim of modernizing Britain to make it a strong and confident democracy in the 21st century', and that was enough for Tory Chairman Michel Ancram, who accused Cherie of acting as an apologist for her husband and his government. He put Conservative Rottweiler John Bercow on the case and Bercow described Cherie as 'an unaccountable cross between First Lady and Lady Macbeth', once again trying to demonstrate that Cherie was a left-wing metropolitan trendy who was having an undue influence on her husband's politics.

There wasn't a shred of evidence to support this. What was more interesting was that Cherie had started a new business timed to coincide with the new human rights legislation introduced by her husband's government. There were no state secrets involved, but it was an interesting insight into Cherie's career. She seemed determined to make it very clear publicly that she was going to press on with her own work and earn as much money as she could, regardless of what the government was doing and saying. Perhaps the more interesting question is not 'What influence does Cherie have on Tony?', but 'What influence does Tony's job have on Cherie's career?' How much money was Matrix going to make from human rights cases, and how much work would the new Act bring to Cherie and her colleagues at Matrix?

Martin Mears, a former president of the Law Society, pointed out that while that it was undoubtedly true that Matrix barristers would make money out of the human rights cases they took on, making money was not the only thing. There was a high profile for lawyers in the human rights field and this attracted people to it as much as, if not more than, the financial gains. Now firmly in the public eye as First Lady of the United Kingdom, Cherie wanted to increase her profile as a barrister to match. She had been determined, when she boarded the train at Lime Street Station in Liverpool to travel to London for the first time nearly thirty years before, that hard work and her own brilliance were going to take her to the top of whichever tree she chose to climb.

The 2001 General Election had been planned for 2 May, which suited Tony and suited Cherie. She would spend the whole of the campaign at Tony's side, and then she would go to court for a gruelling case where she would be appearing for ICI.

But because of the foot-and-mouth epidemic which overtook Britain in 2001, the election was postponed to 7 June. There was no chance that Cherie could get her court case postponed, so Tony, who was desperately keen to have his wife by his side, had to manage without her except for the weekends and a week when the court didn't sit for half term. There could have been no better demonstration of how independently the Blairs worked, and there could have been no better example of Cherie taking a case where she was on the opposite side of the courtroom from the very people Labour wanted to vote for them in the election.

Cherie was defending ICI against more than 400 former workers who claimed that the chemicals giant broke agreements on pay and pensions. The workers, who were transferred in 1994 from ICI's Central Engineering Services on Teesside to Kvaerner Engineering, claim that they lost their security of employment, and that a promised fourteen per cent pay rise failed to materialize. They also allege that their pensions were eroded by the change.

Each of the workers invested thousands of pounds to launch the High Court action, and they employed Antonio Bueno QC to speak for them. They were claiming around £100m in compensation.

Cherie Booth argued in court that none of the workers was worse off through being employed by Kvaerner, while many were better off. 'The company is refuting the case being brought against it quite vigorously, and fully expects to see its point upheld,' said a spokesman for ICI.

The workers, who were claiming misrepresentation and breach of contract, all worked for a maintenance group which looked after ICI plants at Wilton, Billingham and North Tees.

At one time there were 2,000 workers involved, but as ICI shed its Teesside manufacturing base it sought to offload the engineers in an attempt to save the remaining 461 jobs in 1994.

Cherie Booth QC told Mr Justice Elias: 'ICI felt there was a cancer of overtime culture.'

Because journalists were busy with the election, and because what was going on in Court Number 72 at the Courts of Justice was dry stuff involving trolley loads of papers and legal texts,

Cherie got little attention for the work she was doing. Day after day she was appearing in Court representing a multinational while her husband was touring the country trying to persuade workers to vote for his government. There coudn't be a better example of the way Cherie has developed her career entirely independent of her husband and his government and at the end of his first four years she seemed to be doing it very successfully.

Thirteen
SOMEBODY'S MOTHER

The Blairs have made much of their determination to allow their children to grow up in private, even though they live at 10 Downing Street. A deal was agreed with the press shortly after Blair became Prime Minister. The children would be allowed to go about their daily lives unphotographed and unremarked. In return for this there would be an annual Blair family photocall.

Cherie was only too aware of the problems of having a famous father and she wanted to protect her kids from what she had suffered herself. She loved her dad and later forgave him, but she hated the way he had treated her mother. She knew that Tony Blair would have a different relationship with the press, but she realized that if her kids were anything like her they would hate to see their dad's name in the papers whatever the reason. Cherie felt that most kids disliked the reflected light of their parents' fame shining on them. But she also said she didn't want them to get any false ideas of their own importance. 'I don't want my children growing up thinking they are special just because of what their daddy does.'

But these were future plans. The Blairs had to get to Downing Street first. Like all politicians in search of votes they played up their image as a wholesome young family. That meant showing off the kids now and then.

In July 1994 while he was canvassing to become leader of the Labour Party Tony Blair had invited ITN to his home in Richmond Crescent. Lots of film was shot in a local park. Tony Blair demonstrated his football skills with Euan and Nicky and a couple of their friends. The family nanny Ros Mark stood on the sidelines ready to take the boys back home when the photo opportunity was over.

There was also a brief and very rare interview with Tony and Cherie by Michael Brunson, who was then ITN's Political Editor. Brunson wrote in his autobiography *A Ringside Seat*:

> Cherie became sufficiently relaxed to admit quite openly that she was indeed greatly looking forward to the prospect of life at 10 Downing Street, should it ever happen. Even as she was uttering the words I could sense Tony Blair's considerable unease that his wife appeared to be mentally measuring up the curtains for the Prime Ministerial flat, before he had even been elected leader of the Labour Party.
>
> I begged for one last shot inside their home, and with considerable reluctance they agreed. It turned out to be just what we wanted. Their son Euan as well as being good at football also turned out to be rather good at playing the piano, though all requests to Tony Blair himself to remind us of his prowess on the guitar fell on deaf ears. In the street outside however as we prepared to leave, he could no longer contain his anxieties about the whole operation, and especially about the interview with Cherie. He quietly suggested a deal – that we should use the pictures of Euan at the piano in return for not using Cherie's remarks about Number 10.

Brunson agreed to Blair's skilful news management, using Euan to protect his mum Cherie. He thought Cherie's remarks were innocuous, and it was not worth losing the sequence around the piano.

Later that year Euan Blair got his second blast of public attention. The Blairs, like parents everywhere had to choose a secondary school for him. In 1994 choice of schools was the middle-class, Labour voting London parents' worst dilemma.

Endless north London dinner parties were spent discussing whether or not to put one's children before one's principles. Principles seldom won. The Blairs didn't even seem to hesitate. The children and their future come first said Tony.

The press discovered the Blairs were trying to get Euan into the London Oratory School, a selective and grant maintained state school in Fulham. It had opted out of local authority control under Conservative government reforms which Labour had opposed. The Oratory runs a series of interviews with parents and potential pupils before they decide which boys they will select. Euan Blair was amongst the chosen ones.

'They always wanted a Catholic School,' said Margaret Hodge MP who was at that time the Blairs' neighbour in Richmond Crescent. 'It was always going to be the London Oratory or the Cardinal Vaughan near Holland Park.'

Other friends reported that Cherie was amazed and very cross when there was a public outcry about Euan's future. Both Blairs noted carefully that if they wanted to keep the kids out of the limelight, decisions about their futures would have to be kept as low key as possible. But there was an election to win first.

As May 1997 approached, Tony Blair spoke about his children a great deal and several pictures of the family were released to the press. 'The three women in my life' an exclusive article by Tony Blair appeared in *Woman* magazine in early 1997:

> My daughter Kathryn has my mother's red hair and her second name is Hazel after my mum. She's a gorgeous girl with a great personality – sweet and strong willed. We've always tried to treat her the same as the boys but she's so different and has always been completely uninterested in their passion for football. She went straight for the dolls. I think all fathers dote on their daughters and it's lovely to have a girl in the house.

There were six family photographs with the article, including Kathryn aged three with her daddy, a portrait of the whole family together and a specially posed three-shot of Gale, Cherie and Kathryn.

There was one member of the Blair household who stayed out of the limelight during all the election publicity: Ros Mark, the family's nanny. The public's first glimpse of her was on 3 May 1997 when she supervised the move to Downing Street. She was seen struggling out the front door of Richmond Crescent with piles of suitcases and racks of Cherie's shoes. She was an attractive and casually dressed thirty-year-old blonde who adopted the modern teenage style of unlaced sneakers, sweatshirt and jeans. She looked friendly and approachable and very much in the style of the new government.

Once the Blair family *en masse* were safely installed at Number 10 where they spent a few cramped weeks before taking over Gordon Brown's larger and more comfortable place at Number 11, the shutters were drawn and all publicity ceased. Ros Mark was asked to sign a retrospective confidentiality agreement, which meant that she had agreed not to talk about her experiences with the family right back to the time she joined them three years before. The co-signatory to the agreement was Cherie. The new arrangements for the press and the children were re-emphasized and it was stressed again that Cherie, when she was not playing her public role of Mrs Blair and out on official business at her husband's side, was to be left in peace.

Like Cherie, Ros Mark came from Liverpool. They had other things in common. Ros came from a broken home. Her father had walked out on the family when Ros was only eight. Ros was clever. She passed the entrance exam for an exclusive independent school. Her mother didn't have much money so Ros benefited from the assisted places scheme. She got 10 'O' levels, left school and went as a trainee to Barclays Bank. But the bank was too dull and repetitive for such a bright spark and she soon left to see the world. She started out as an au pair in Perth. Later she took a nursery nurse course at a Montessori college in London. In 1994 she took a job as nanny to a busy young north London professional couple, Tony and Cherie Blair.

For the Blairs Ros was a godsend. Bright, intelligent and funny, she soon became an essential element in their busy lives. Tony had become the party leader and Cherie was now a QC. The family were desperately busy and appreciative of the important support role Ros had begun to play. Blair friends spoke of how well she fitted in, Blair neighbours observed wryly that she became the family's representative in relationships with other residents of the Crescent. One neighbour described her as 'a tough cookie. An expert at defending the Blairs' rights.' The Blairs were so busy that the other members of Ros's family, her mother Margaret and her brother were sometimes called in as emergency helpers. Margaret and Ros took the Blair children to the family home in Lancashire when the Blairs were particularly hard pressed. Margaret Mark says, 'Nobody knew who Ros worked for. She never mentioned it to our neighbours. We had the Blair children up to stay for the holidays, we took them to Blackpool and nobody knew who they were. They played outside the house with Ros, they played football and nobody knew who they were. She didn't tell anybody. She was so protective of the Blairs.'

The Mark family live in Galgate, an old Lancashire village with lots of new building just off the M6 on the outskirts of Lancaster. Their estate, Crofters Fold, is neat, silent and modern. There are few people at home in the daytime. Knock on ten doors and you would be lucky to find one young mother with a babe in arms. The Mark residence is immaculate. Lawn neatly clipped, flowerbed watered, soil turned over to a regulation tilth. The house is small and see-through. From the window by the front door it's possible to examine the equally neat back garden. Here the young Blairs played with the neighbours, safely watched over by Ros a world away from 10 Downing Street

Keen as she was on the family Ros gave up working for them at the end of the summer of 1998. Tony had been Prime Minister for eighteen months. The Blairs encouraged Ros to develop her skills and talents and get herself a real career. She applied to do a teacher training course in Lancaster and started at college in the autumn. The Blairs kept in touch because they were very fond of Ros and appreciated what she and her family had done for them at a very important time in their lives.

The relationships between the Blairs and their former nanny changed for ever on Saturday 4 March 2000. For forty-eight hours after that day, the silent streets of Crofters Fold became home to the British media who set up camp outside the Mark's neat front door.

The Prime Minister's spokesman Alastair Campbell was on a train to Burnley that Saturday morning to watch his favourite football team when he was telephoned by Ros Mark. Ros was upset. She told Campbell that she had written a kind of diary of her time with the Blairs, the story of the effect of life at the top on an ordinary person like herself. 'Somehow she thought, however naïvely, that her account would be a nice piece of social history about growing up in a family that suddenly was living in Downing Street,' said Campbell.

Ros's mother Margaret explained later that it had all come about when Ros had started at college, she had attended a history lecture and the teacher had stressed the importance of 'oral history'. Ros then appears to have had the idea that she had something to contribute in this area. Her mother explained that Ros had thought, 'I was an ordinary person living at an extraordinary address and I really would like to write how I felt when I was living there, what I found. The Blairs were bit players in it because obviously she mentioned them but certainly it wasn't The Archers of Downing Street.'

Ros Mark then appears to have produced a mammoth 180,000-word tome about life and times with the Blairs. This piece of dynamite was offered to an agent who apparently told Ros that its domestic contents would not sell unless she could add some sex and kiss-and-tell to the mix.

Ros told Alastair Campbell when she phoned him that Saturday morning that she believed that the whole idea of doing the book was off, but somehow the *Mail on Sunday* were planning to publish a story about her tomorrow, and frankly she was worried. Campbell certainly didn't seem to be worried at this stage. He told Ros to get in touch with the editor of the *Mail on Sunday* and get him to confirm by fax that any deal was off. He went on to watch his home team Burnley lose 3-0 and didn't think about Ros and her Nanny's Tale again until he got a call from the *Mail on Sunday* at quarter to six in the afternoon. He had a friendly conversation with the paper over its plans to publish a story about Ros's memoirs. Simon Walters, the paper's political editor who sees Campbell nearly every day, did not – at least according to Downing Street – let on that the paper had seen the book. Both Downing Street and the *Mail on Sunday* described the talks as 'relaxed' with Alastair Campbell raising no objection about the paper's intentions.

There was no reason for Campbell to believe that Ros would have betrayed their trust, according to another friend of the Blairs. 'Ros was a very friendly and sociable person who got on really well with the children. It is difficult to imagine her doing anything like this. Their nannies are extremely close to them. They are very much part of the set and are treated very well.'

Confident that it had secured Campbell's blessing for the project, the newspaper contacted Ros again and, according to its statement, was offered the rights to serialize her book. At best there appears to have been a misunderstanding between the *Mail on Sunday* and Downing Street. The paper believed that it would face no objections for serializing the book whose disclosures – which ran in the first five editions – were more affectionate than damaging. Alastair Campbell, according to Downing Street, believed that he had only given his blessing to the paper writing a story about Ros having written her memoirs.

As he returned to London by car, the *Mail on Sunday*'s presses rolled and 1.5 million copies were printed. By the time Campbell saw the paper's first edition when it was delivered to his house in London about ten o'clock in the evening he was horrified. There was a double page spread of Ros's revelations. The *Mail on Sunday*'s headlines said it revealed a 'nanny's view of life with the Blair family'.

'It was far more serious than I was led to believe,' Campbell said.

Cherie was in London and Tony was in his Sedgefield constituency when Alastair Campbell got moving on what was to become later the first great sign of the Blair's absolute determination to control their own private lives and those of their children. Campbell set up a conference call linking the Blairs with himself and the Blair's old friend Lord Falconer who was now a government minister as well as a lawyer. They agreed to seek an injunction on Cherie's behalf if they could not persuade the paper to halt publication.

Alastair Campbell phoned Jonathan Harris, the agent Ros had approached with her book, and asked him three times whether he had played a part in the *Mail on Sunday*'s disclosures. Harris, who according to Downing Street did not provide any explanation about the disclosures, issued a statement denying any involvement in events of the past few days, insisting that he had ended his relationship with Ros Mark.

Meanwhile another Blair family friend Val Davies, a solicitor with Norton Rose, spoke to Eddie Young, the *Mail on Sunday*'s night lawyer, and other of the paper's executives, before getting the legal machinery into gear. The Blairs are surrounded by close friends and contacts in the law and were able to act very quickly indeed. They arranged to raise Mr Justice Jackson's clerk at around 1.15 a.m. Five minutes later the paper was told an injunction was being sought. The judge was approached directly at 1.30 a.m. and, within fifteen minutes, an injunction was granted. The decision was relayed to the paper at 1.58 a.m. and, after the *Mail on Sunday* failed to persuade the judge to lift the injunction, the presses were stopped.

Cherie Booth, seven months pregnant, upset and furious, went off to bed. She couldn't believe that Ros who had been so close to her could have betrayed her, as she saw it, so comprehensively.

At the Mark home in Galgate all hell was about to break loose.

'I have had my fingers burned by this experience,' said Miss Mark. 'I'm absolutely devastated that something I wanted to be nice about the Blairs and my time with them has been presented in the way that it has and has caused them upset.' Her mother Margaret said that the family had been phoned by Downing Street and told not to speak to the press, and not to go out. 'We were stupidly naïve to believe what Downing Street said – that they would put out press statements and tell the story as it was. Now for one reason or another that never happened. I'm not saying they didn't put out the press statements but obviously the press were more interested in hearing from Ros than they were from Alastair Campbell.

'We had the press camped outside all day Sunday. When we came downstairs in the morning we found them all outside. We literally crawled into the kitchen on our hands and knees and took the kettle from the workbench and a packet of Ryvita biscuits and the butter from the fridge and we went with a packet of tea bags into the back room and there we lived for the rest of the day.

'Tony rang on the Sunday morning when this broke and he promised us he would help us over this dreadful issue. He believed that Ros hadn't done anything wrong and he rang again later in the evening to find out how she was and said that she must carry on as normal. That poor kid went out at seven the next morning running the gauntlet of all the press and TV cameras, to catch the coach to go to her school practice and she said nothing to them because she believed that Downing Street and Tony would tell the world that she had done nothing wrong. But we were completely on our own.'

What Ros didn't understand was that she was now outside the Blairs' protective cordon. She seemed to believe she was still on the same side as Tony. When she'd called Alastair Campbell she was asking for help and hoping that he would protect her from the press the way he had done when she was at Downing Street. Somehow she seemed to believe that Campbell would sort out the mess on her behalf. She seemed to have a touching belief that if Tony Blair said things would be OK, then they'd be OK.

On the Friday of the same week the situation was resolved for Ros. A high court judge upheld an injunction preventing the *Mail on Sunday* publishing details of her memoirs. Just hours before the hearing, Mrs Blair had announced that she was dropping the claim for damages from Ros if she returned any copies of the manuscript she still had in her possession. Mr Justice Morland rejected the application by Associated Newspapers, publishers of the *Mail on Sunday*, to overturn the injunction granted to Cherie Blair on the Sunday. In his ruling, the judge said that Mrs Blair, who was seven months pregnant, had already suffered sleepless nights because she was fearful of the effects publication of Miss Mark's story would have on her family and that to lift the injunction now was only likely to cause increased distress to Mrs Blair.

The judge also said that the newspaper must have been aware that by publishing Miss Mark's account it was putting her in breach of a private confidentiality agreement she had signed with the Blairs.

The Blairs said they were happy with the ruling. Number 10 said: 'The Prime Minister accepts the legitimate scrutiny of him and his actions and he and Mrs Blair also accept there will be a great deal of media interest in their lives. But they will continue to protect their children from unwarranted intrusion and to ensure they grow up in a trusting, secure family environment.'

A joint statement was issued on behalf of Cherie and Ros. In it Cherie accepted that Ros Mark had not sent a 450-page manuscript detailing her life with the Blairs to the *Mail on Sunday* newspaper.

There is no doubt that Ros Mark was naïve if she didn't realize that the story of her life with the Blairs, in whatever form it was written, would generate huge public interest. The battle over her diaries and the Blairs' victory was an important signal to the media from Downing Street that all incursions into the Blair's family life would be dealt with severely who ever they came from.

The next great family news event was the birth of Leo Blair. Fresh from his triumph in 'Nannygate', Alastair Campbell boasted that he would get Cherie from Downing Street to the Chelsea and Westminster Hospital and back again without a usable picture being taken. He succeeded. Apart from Mary McCartney's official photos from inside Number 10 the only public sighting of Leo was as a small bundle in his father's arms when the family moved to Chequers for ten days Prime Ministerial paternity leave. Surprisingly it was to be sixteen-year-old Euan who provided the next opportunity for legitimate discussion of the private life of the Blairs.

The nation collectively choked on its toast when the story of Euan's drunken episode was revealed on morning radio. It had only been a few days since Tony Blair's government had come up with the idea that boozed up yobs should be hauled to cash point machines to pay instant fines for their misdemeanours. Of course I felt sorry for Euan. Everybody deserves to make their first few mistakes in private. All MP's children know the horror of getting their name in the paper for some small incident just because dad is a local celebrity. Our own daughter Hannah who had gone to sleep leaving a candle burning too near her bed, had managed to set our house in Grimsby on fire. She was interviewed about her adventure on radio after several fire engines had arrived and the whole family in night attire had been removed to the safety of the street. Humiliated by having to confess her sins in public, she wouldn't discuss the incident again for years. I decided to give her a ring so that she could commiserate with Euan. She hadn't heard the news, so I told her the story in detail. 'That's funny', she said: 'Anne [her best friend in the office] discovered an unconscious teenager lying against a wall in Leicester Square last night . . .'

Anne Davis is a young widow. When the Euan incident happened she had been on one of her few nights out since her husband Alan's funeral. He'd died, very young, of cancer and they hadn't been married long. Anne and her friend Lyndsey had been to the cinema and were walking home when they saw a young man covered in vomit lying close to a wall. To Anne, who was at this stage of her life particularly sensitive, he looked either dead or very ill. She also noticed that the lad was very young looking and he wasn't wearing the kind of clothes that distinguish perpetual Leicester Square drunks. Lyndsey and Anne went in search of a policeman. It took them quite a while. They had to walk to the nearest station, queue up and then attract the interest on the person on duty. The police took quite a bit of convincing. 'He'll just be a vagrant', said the desk man. Drunks lying in the street are not a high priority in central London. Anne and Lyndsey were persuasive and eventually a policeman was dispatched with them to find the young man. He was still lying in the same place. Passers-by were carefully walking round him. Anne and her mate made sure the boy was safe with the police and went on their way.

As Hannah was telling me this story we both began to realize that there were hardly likely to have been two young middle-class drunks lying in Leicester Square on the same evening. Anne was brought into the conversation and we all realized simultaneously that the boy Anne had helped in Leicester Square had been Euan Blair.

Anne's story was in the papers the next day. Interest was intense. When journalists first found out what had happened they weren't sure whether they could even report the story because of the agreement the Blairs had with them about no publicity for the children. But then Downing Street put out a statement which effectively sanctioned reporters to go ahead and talk about it. Adam Boulton, Sky's political correspondent and one of the first to hear the news, wondered how he should treat the story.

'You think to yourself, is this politically significant? What are the questions that are asked? How hard or self-righteous, or whatever, should you be? And you just have to take a judgement at that point because that's the nature of twenty-four hour news. I was one of the first people telling the story and I said, "in the end we've all been teenagers".'

What Boulton didn't know when he decided to take a sympathetic line with Euan's plight was that Cherie was watching his report on Sky in the British Ambassador's home in Portugal. 'Of course they are going to draw conclusions about you on the basis of what you say, and they decide how they will relate to you in future.' As it happens, he and Cherie had always got on well, and Adam felt this incident increased her warmness towards him.

Tony Blair appeared on *Question Time* on BBC Television the following evening. The programme started badly for the Prime Minister, but that was inevitable. The very first question from a fellow barrister was about the arrest of Euan. 'Who should be dragged to the cash machine to pay the hundred pound fine, the father or the son?', asked Christian Mole. During the question Tony Blair was tight-lipped and groping for control. At one stage he drew his lips back and his teeth chattered. He explained that the law must be applied to his family as well as everyone else in Britain and that if his son had broken the law then he had to pay the penalty. He was on the edge of tears when he muttered: 'I guess that most of us at the age of sixteen has done things they regret. Not everyone has to see it the next day in the papers.' Then he began to burble. 'I don't know what behaviour he did . . .' He was clearly shocked and in pain. A woman in a pink T-shirt was called to speak. Instead of asking a question she tried to comfort the Prime Minister. 'Your son was behaving in a normal way,' she said, and the audience clapped and cheered to show that they too felt sorry for this father and son in trouble.

There were references to Euan's binge throughout the programme and each time the Prime Minister looked really upset and on edge. He seized on questions about the political issues of the day with all the relief of a patient in the dentist's chair when the drilling stops and they're offered a glass of mouthwash.

Both Tony and Cherie had been shown in different ways that journalists and the public can be sympathetic and understanding if left to make up their own minds. But the Euan incident marked the lowest period of Blair's first term. The Prime Minister seemed to have lost his magic touch and there was a severe nose dive in the opinion polls. It turned out to be temporary, but at the time it looked as if late nights, nappy changing, and dealing with a tenacious public interest in his family life were taking their toll.

Cherie on the other hand was flourishing. She seemed tougher, more resilient and more in control than her husband. She wrote warmly to Anne Davis: 'Dear Anne, Thank you so much for what you did for Euan in Leicester Square. You were definitely a Good Samaritan' – and gained another life member for the growing Cherie Booth supporter's club.

Forced onto the back foot for a week or two by Euan Blair's burst of self-generated publicity, the Downing Street machine was soon back on form when Baby Leo started going out and about with his mum. Cherie went to give support to the Labour candidate and fellow barrister David Lammy in the Tottenham by-election. Leo was in the car with his nanny and some pooled ITN footage of the visit accidentally revealed Leo's big toe peeping out the end of his carry-cot. Broadcasters were puzzled and amazed when officials at Number 10 protested at what they claimed had been 'a gross breach of privacy rules'. Most people who saw the footage didn't even spot the toe and Downing Street was forced to retreat.

The next battle front was opened on Sedgefield Green at the end of July when Leo made his first visit to his father's constituency for his christening. There were no pictures from inside the tiny church of St John Fisher but all the Sunday papers carried shots of the baby in Cherie's arms outside the church. Number 10 initially claimed that this too had breached the Press Complaints commission privacy rules and threatened to call in the watchdog to investigate the incident. Officials said that they had specifically asked the media to stay away from Sedgefield.

It was an interesting dilemma. Was there a Leo line over which journalists could not venture without permission from Number 10? Did the baby's presence at any public event mean that the Blairs could order the press to stay away?

Alastair Campbell huffed and puffed and admitted that the pictures from Sedgefield were inoffensive, but emphasized once again the Blairs did not want to start an open season on photographs of their children. A spokesman for the newspaper industry said that any complaint to the Commission would have been thrown out. 'It's a joke. They were in a public place at an event which had been trailed in advance by Downing Street.'

Then school teacher Andria Fannon took a snap of Cherie and Leo at Durham Cricket Club in Chester Le Street. Cherie had fetched Leo from the car where he was waiting with his nanny. Pupils from St John's Roman Catholic comprehensive school gathered round Cherie and the baby for ten minutes. Andria took some pictures and sent one to the local newspaper for a round-up of school news, a regular feature which duly appeared a few days later. Local people teased Andria that she had broken the rules, and out of interest she rang Downing Street and told them what she had done. She was given a severe dressing down by an official and made to understand that she had committed a serious offence. The *Darlington Echo* took up Andria's case and once again realizing that they looked foolish, Downing Street retreated mumbling, 'We are very anxious that these photos should not be reprinted and that the Blair's privacy is respected.'

After that Leo's first year continued in relative peace. When he was around six months old a clown was entertaining children at a Downing Street party and Cherie brought Leo outside to watch. The papers all carried a picture the next morning and Downing Street, which had presumably learned something from its previous over-the-top reactions, said nothing at all.

As the election approached attitudes to press coverage of the Blair family became noticeably more relaxed. Politicians across Britain were dusting down their wives and getting their children's hair cut in preparation. The Blair children appeared several times with their parents. Euan now sixteen and a member of the Labour Party was seen at a rally with his mum and a girlfriend. Kathryn and Nicky went canvassing with their dad, but they'd become less of a draw card now Leo was around.

All the family except Leo were photographed crossing the meadow in front of Myrobella, Blair's home in Trimdon Colliery, on the morning of election day. All of them turned up for the counting of dad's votes on election night where they were filmed walking and chatting together. Only Kathryn who is just the wrong age to feel comfortable in public, looked shy. Then the next day they appeared on the steps of 10 Downing Street for a victory photograph call. The boys were in suits and businessmen's ties. Kathryn wore a droopy floor length frock, and Leo's little cardigan was ironed to perfection. You couldn't help admiring a father who had managed to persuade his brood to dress in such an extraordinary fashion, even if they were all back in their jeans and T-shirts the minute the front door closed.

In all their pleas for privacy, the Blairs insist that it is their children's lives they are protecting. They want them to be given the chance to grow up as normally as possible. Few people would disagree with such reasonable aims.

The Blair Government has begun its second term, and the Blairs themselves are seen to be even more powerful and distant from the ordinary lives they so crave for their children. They live in a style and with a level of protection more usual for American Presidents than British Prime Ministers. Cherie Booth is still Ms Booth in private and Mrs Blair in public, but even some of her work as Prime Minister's wife is now conducted under controlled conditions when it suits her and her Downing Street minders.

During the 2001 election campaign Fiona Millar begged a Channel 4 News cameraman doing a report on party leaders' wives to come and spend as much time as he liked filming Cherie. He was allowed access to her Chambers, to receptions at Downing Street and as many events as he wanted to choose on the Blair's British election tour.

Six weeks later, after the election was duly won, the Blairs made an official visit to South America where Cherie had her own programme. Travelling in the footsteps of Princess Diana, she visited an orphanage in Rio de Janeiro, talked to street children in Sao Paulo and women convicted of drug offences in St Augusta prison in Jamaica. Downing Street described her schedule as 'private' and banned the British press from following her. They defended her right to make the visits 'in private' although she was accompanied by local journalists. 'She doesn't want to turn everything into a jamboree,' said the Downing Street spokesperson.

When we see Mrs Cherie Blair touring South America it is not just the good works and the glamorous outfits which remind us of Princess Diana. Cherie is emulating Diana's love–hate relationship with the press. She needs them, but she hates them being there. It caused Princess Diana more pain than any other aspect of her life in her final years. Cherie seems uncertain now where her public and private lives intersect. She has begun to expect a right to a private life in public places just like Diana did.

In the week Mrs Blair was paying her private visits to orphanages, street children and jails in South America the TV presenter Anna Ford lost her High Court bid to overturn a Press Complaints Commission ruling over paparazzi pictures of her in a bikini. The PCC ruled that the pictures did not amount to an invasion of privacy because she was on a public beach overlooked by apartments. Ford, however, said she had an expectation of privacy because she was on a secluded section of the beach.

Cherie too seems to want to control the beach, to establish her right to control the situation whether she's in public or in her sitting room in the Downing Street flat. Mrs Blair, like Anna Ford, is a public person. It's fine to demand and get privacy for your children but it's hard to see that public figures, especially those who are there because British people voted for the political party their husband leads, should be dealt the same privileges.

Fourteen

THE MANY FRIENDS OF MRS BLAIR

When Tony Blair became Prime Minister his wife and children found themselves in an unusual situation. There was no escape route, they had no family hideaway within reach of the places they worked and went to school where they could retreat to if the going got tough. The Blair and Booth parents all live in modest and crowded cottages scattered across England so there was no parental bolthole where they could store the baggage that every family collects – the boxes of old school books, the spare tennis rackets, the relics of youthful passions for karate or kickboxing. The Blairs had nowhere they could escape occasionally from the public eye – unlike previous Prime Ministers and their families. John and Norma Major had a place which really was their home in Huntingdon, Harold and Mary Wilson kept their family house in Hampstead Garden Suburb through the whole of his leadership, but the Blairs sold up and moved everything to Number 10 Downing Street. All their possessions, from Cherie's shoe collection to Tony's guitar and Vera Booth's bed were squeezed into a small flat in Westminster.

All their old friends and neighbours were gone and they found themselves surrounded with a whole lot of new people who were destined to get to know them and become close to them whether the Blairs wanted new friends or not. The press and the media, the control of whom has become so important to the Blairs, were literally camped on the front doorstep so the Blairs did something about it.

Together they created for themselves a private stockade, a premium laager at the heart of the British Government, where admission is strictly by invitation only. The gatekeepers have regularly updated lists of those who are allowed instant access – a very élite band, most of them the tested and tried few who have been with the Blairs from the start. It's unlikely to include key cabinet colleagues like the Deputy Prime Minister John Prescott or Margaret Beckett. It's bound to feature celebrities whose company the Blairs enjoy. Princess Strozzi was one of the first visitors after the birth of Leo. Tony would be unlikely to turn down a chat with Sir Paul McCartney or Sir Alex Ferguson. Peter Mandelson is no longer in the laager and doesn't fit with the old ease, but old habits are hard to break and he is said to ring regularly for a chat. He certainly likes to give the impression that he's still in the inner circle even if his is now a country membership. Until the court case over her memoirs, Rosalind Mark, the Blair's ex-nanny was encouraged to call the Prime Minister at any time. She had spoken to him only days before the story broke.

The other people with real access are first and foremost the Blair family. Cherie's mum Gale spends most of her time at Downing Street looking after her grandchildren. Tony's dad Leo, Cherie's sister Lyndsey and Tony's brother Bob are all kept in touch. The inner circle of close friends and advisers who are welcome at any time include all the old ones, like the Lords Irvine and Falconer and Jonathan Powell and a clutch of judges, barristers and solicitors including Maggie Rae and Val Davies who are mates of Cherie. Anji Hunter, Blair's closest personal aide and of course the ubiquitous Campbell Millars, the gatekeepers. The Blairs' most trusted friends these days are blood relations, old friends who have stayed trustworthy and the people who work with them and around them – the people whose job it is to keep others away.

James Hughes-Onslow, an old friend of the couple who attended their wedding but who works as a journalist with the London *Evening Standard*, tried to explain to Fiona Millar that he would not do anything as a journalist to hurt Cherie because he was her friend. 'You are an old friend, not a new friend,' Fiona said icily. Journalists are not on the trusted list.

Troublesome relatives like Tony Booth, Cherie's father, who has a habit of turning up unexpectedly at his daughter's photo-opportunities, and the journalist Lauren Booth, Cherie's half-sister, are mistrusted as opportunists trying to use their relations with the first family for their own purposes. They are kept carefully outside the stockade; their access is rationed. Just enough to keep them loyal, little enough to starve them of information about what's really going on inside.

When life is tough – and no one denies Cherie's life is tough, working hard as a barrister on the treadmill, bringing up a large family and supporting and directing a Prime Ministerial husband – then being protected from the outside world can be an important part of why and how you can manage. It helps Cherie enormously that she can be so largely insulated against the day-to-day stresses and strains, the hassles and abrasions of the real world that more ordinary mortals must survive. The absolute loyalty of her friends is important too. Most people who have even the smallest part to play in her busy life feel that they owe her total loyalty. Friends who become a bit over enthusiastic about their access can be gently or crudely distanced from the inner circle depending on the seriousness of their transgressions. This sort of tough management is hard to combine with the image of the Prime Minister's wife cultivated during elections and at other times of Blairite need. But with part-time access available to an increasing number of celebrities, and to a few of the rich and powerful who are familiar with the problem themselves and have the power to provide the insulation and exclusivity which Cherie most needs to continue her double life, it will be hard for her to go on playing two such contrasting roles for much longer.

Those with access to the laager are regularly vetted, their performance as loyalists assessed and failures are harshly dealt with. Lord Winston, Professor of Fertility Studies at Hammersmith Hospital London was a great favourite. He was made a peer but then in an interview published in the *New Statesman* magazine when the journalist Mary Riddell mentioned Chelsea and Westminster Hospital, Lord Winston said: 'Oh, that's where Cherie Blair is having her Caesarean section.' In the event, the Caesarean section wasn't necessary, but the fact that he had spoken to journalists about something as private as Cherie's pregnancy got him into a lot of trouble. There were telephone calls between Number 10, Fiona, Alastair Campbell and a worried Winston, who is no longer a trusty.

Again during Cherie's pregnancy, Bharti Vhyas, the ayurvedic therapist, talked to the press and mentioned that Cherie was her client. This was true and Cherie is still on her client list, but Vhyas was forced to retract and the BBC, who had published the information, had to come up with an apology. Paddy Campbell, the dress designer who supplies many of Cherie's clothes these days is terrified to say anything at all about her famous client in case she loses her custom. Carol Chaplin who was Cherie's lifestyle and clothes adviser at the beginning of her period as leader's wife, is now a fitness instructor with the Holmes Place gym in central London. Even though she is still trying to make a living as a fitness and lifestyle adviser she too is very apprehensive about what would happen if she talked about her relationship with Cherie.

When Cherie discovered a documentary was being made about her by Channel 4, she immediately called her old pal and Deputy Chairman of Channel 4 Barry Cox who told the Commissioning Editor concerned that Cherie was worried about people upsetting her friends in 'my home town' (Liverpool). Cox managed to suggest lightly to the Channel 4 executive that the production company making the project weren't altogether respectable. He is well aware that it is my production company.

When she is at home at 10 Downing Street, the relationship between Mrs Blair and the press is very close – physically anyway. Westminster is small and crowded. Most events happen in a political triangle marked by the Millbank Tower, Downing Street and Victoria Station. Downing Street is the apex and the media people who belong to the parliamentary lobby spend their working lives here. They are often the first and the last people the Blair family see every day because they work inside the iron gates which cut Downing Street off from the rest of the world. Their workstation is just outside the front door of Number 10. There is usually someone recording a contribution to a news programme, filming a visiting delegation or shouting at the ministers trekking in and out. Cherie gets to know the regulars on her doorstep very well indeed

The political editor of Sky News, Adam Boulton, sees a lot of Cherie. If the Prime Minister is on a trip overseas and she is accompanying him, then Adam and Cherie might have a great deal of contact over a short space of time. They will be travelling together, sharing their reactions to the events on the tour. If something goes wrong with the programme they might joke about it together. If something is very moving or very funny they might exchange a comment. When they are at home, day to day, Cherie uses the front door of Number 10. She goes in and out of her home, to the gym, to work or shopping. Adam reports on the main political story of the day so he will be standing outside the front door as Cherie comes and goes.

'One of the things the Blairs have been very successful with is establishing this demarcation line. We can film her, but we don't film her when she is with the children. She knows she can be filmed at any time and she'll wave to the photographers she recognizes.'

There's a special relationship between the Westminster lobby and Cherie: they both know and play by the rules. She never does any interviews or gives her opinion on anything outside the strict confines of her legal work or her charity work. The press never photograph her when she's rushing off to the gym without make-up at eight o'clock in the morning.

Boulton thinks Cherie has become very good at working with the press and now she is demonstrating an easy, relaxed relationship with members of the public. 'Tony is a diffident public schoolboy in a lot of situations. There was one time during the 2001 General Election where he was visiting the sports centre at a comprehensive school, and the immediate comparison that came to mind was that he was like Prince Charles, sort of saying, "I had every facility when I was at school. I was very lucky..." He just did not appear to be connecting, whereas Cherie, with her background, is absolutely at home flirting with builders with their tops off and singing along with the Darby and Joan Club. She's very direct with journalists too. She'll just come up and say something mildly flirtatious but within the bounds and connect immediately.'

The politicians down the road in the Palace of Westminster also surround Cherie, but she really only sees the ones who visit her home at Number 10. Just after the 2001 election when Tony was choosing his cabinet, a friend of Cherie's from the old days was called to see the boss to be told of his promotion. Cherie was waiting at the front door. She threw her arms around him and shared the good news before he'd been anywhere near the Prime Minister. It's almost as if life stopped for Cherie the day the Blairs moved into Downing Street. Relationships from before that time have become more precious because she feels she can only trust old friends.

Very occasionally – and these events have to be planned well in advance – Tony and Cherie will make an arrangement to spend the evening with old friends, but this is a special treat for the Blairs and probably imposes quite a strain on the old friends concerned who have to agree to special arrangements and security checks because of who's coming to dinner.

This is the scene on a midweek evening in an expensive outer London suburb when a much planned visit takes place: Three men in their shirt sleeves are sharing a glass of wine and waiting for the latecomers to arrive. They're old friends who first met when they were starting out on their careers, and they have all been successful in their own ways. They don't meet very often. One of the men is the Prime Minister Tony Blair. All the signs of his special presence are kept outside the house. Police cars, flashing lights, security men. Here there is only soft music and reminiscences.

In the kitchen the hostess supervises her staff and talks to a female guest. The hostess is a comparatively new wife and a bit tense. She's shy of the Prime Minister, not having known him in his youth. The men have stuck together, remained the core of the group, friends of Tony. Some of the ex-wives are still friends with the wives who stayed on, but they'd never get together for a reunion like this. The final guest arrives. Cherie, the Prime Minister's wife. The minute she enters the room her husband turns his attention to her. The Blairs are glad to see one another.

Each time they meet the relationship is re-grounded. Tony depends on Cherie. He says often enough 'she is my rock'. Increasingly she is also his connection to the real world. Now that she's conquered her shyness she can chat happily with just about anyone, charming people with her wit, making them feel she's on their level. He finds it much harder to get on with people he's never met before. But tonight they are amongst old friends. Tony kisses Cherie, puts his arm across her shoulder and then rests his hand at the back of her neck. He does this a great deal. They both do. If they are within touching distance they will touch one another in public and in private.

Tony teases Cherie about her visit to the gym. Has she lost another pound or tightened a few more muscles? Then they reinsert themselves into the group. Dinner is served and after a while people forget that this is the Prime Minister and his wife, and they relax and talk and argue just like they always did. Tony is remarkably laid back, listening to what everyone else is saying, asking for their views. Cherie is as usual talkative and trying to persuade Tony he must do something immediately about her latest cause. Around them the talk swirls on. Everyone enjoys the evening and these old friends all vow to meet again very soon, but they know it will be difficult to arrange.

Most of Cherie's oldest friends are the people she works with in the streets around Gray's Inn Road, High Holborn and The Temple. She's been a London lawyer for nearly twenty-five years and here they really do not think of her as the Prime Minister's wife. The woman they know is Cherie Booth QC. Here it's possible to find people who accept her for what she is. One woman lawyer who works with her assured me: 'She's just like the rest of us. I go round to her place to have a chat with her about a case and once you get inside Downing Street it really is just like everyone else's home. The only difference these days is that I quite often have to speak to Fiona Millar before I talk to Cherie instead of going through her clerk.'

In the legal world they can still make jokes with Cherie and tease her about her foibles without expecting it to end up in a diary column. Several people mentioned her driving with affectionate horror. Did I realize, they said, that she is possibly the worst driver in the world? One man told me that he always finds excuses not to travel with Cherie if he is offered a lift. Another says that Cherie trying to pass her driving test was a saga which kept people in her chambers amused for months. 'I remember her coming back once and telling me that the most extraordinary thing had happened. She had so terrified the examiner he'd banged on the dashboard and shouted 'Stop!', jumped out of the car and left her to make her own way back to the test centre.

Whatever her driving skills, for many years driving herself on long journeys was an important part of Cherie's life. Before Tony was the leader of his party the family spent many weekends in the constituency. The Palace of Westminster allows wives and children fifteen free rail journeys to and from the constituency each year. If they want to visit more often it is at their own expense, so Cherie often found herself driving the 250 miles there and 250 miles back every weekend.

Myrobella in Trimdon Colliery at the heart of the Sedgefield constituency is the only home the Blairs own. They don't spend much time there now, perhaps only a handful of nights a year, but the way things are at the moment, if an emergency happened and the Blairs had to leave Downing Street this is the only place that they own that they could run to. Since Tony Blair became Prime Minister there has been a twenty-four-hour guard on the Blairs' house and the police have bought one of the neighbouring properties and turned it into a security station and guard house. Myrobella used to have an open aspect to the fields in front of it and close contact with the cottages behind. It is now completely surrounded by high hedges and security fencing. The local joke its that the crime rate is zero since Tony got to Downing Street because there's so many policemen about.

The village is so small, so intimate, so dominated by the big house at its heart, that it wouldn't be possible to live here and be a Tory.

The Trimdon Colliery residents speak of Cherie much more enthusiastically than they speak of her husband. Tony, they say, is nice enough. He always smiles and waves from his car as he shoots by. He occasionally used to kick a ball around on the green space in front of the cottages with his kids but there's general agreement that he's always been a bit distant, right from the beginning. They don't say so, but you know they mean that he's a nice middle-class man who doesn't really fit in round these parts. They're proud to have a Prime Minister amongst them but you can see he has always been a distant figure and not one of them.

Cherie provokes a much more genuine response. 'She's lovely,' is the usual comment, followed by the fact that she's friendly, ordinary and one of us. Well, was. Everyone agrees that they don't see much of her now.

When Cherie first came to live in Myrobella almost twenty years ago she used the village shop just like everyone else and could be seen walking up the road with her shopping bag. She has been to the shop once since Tony became PM but it was much discussed because she had two security guards with her as she made her way up the main street. I thought this sounded a bit odd for a woman who drives herself to court every day, and goes to out of town court cases and to Liverpool alone on the train, but Trimdon Colliers assure me that this is a true story.

Most of the locals cite Petra Grieves as a bit of an authority on Cherie. Mrs Grieves is the wife of the local butcher Ted. They have a large modern bungalow in the lee of Myrobella. It is so close that it is inside the security cordon which protects the Prime Minister. To get to the butcher's house you have to wait while a policeman in a station examines who you are on the surveillance camera and presses a button to open the big electronic security gates. They do this for everybody, even the residents. There are about three houses on the other side of the gates. There are two sets. It's a bit like the gates on a canal lock. If they change their minds in the police station you could be stuck between the two. The butcher comes home for his dinner in his white van and accepts the security as normal.

Petra is a slim, dark and very attractive woman, not much older than Cherie. Her home is a surprise because it is so different from the small mining cottages at the back. It's cool and spacious and could be in Weybridge or Virginia Water. There's a large mahogany dining table in one room and Conran style sofas in another. The house is private and silent with a gentle lawn ending at a high wall which has been built between the butchers and the Blairs.

Petra and Cherie hit it off immediately when they got together as young mums. Petra's daughter, an attractive young woman in her twenties, lived all of her childhood with the Blairs as her next door neighbours. The Grieves family are guarded about the Blairs, saying only that Cherie is 'marvellous, wonderful and lovely of course'. I explain that her neighbours round the back suggested I should visit her because she has Cherie's dresser to stay when Cherie visits these days. Petra's hand goes straight to her mouth. 'Who told you that?', she says in dismay. I tell her it was one of her neighbours and she looks very nervous. 'She had no right to tell you that. Nobody's supposed to know.' Well, she probably shouldn't have told me, but I am impressed to have it confirmed that Cherie is now taking her public image so seriously that she takes a dresser round the country with her on official occasions. Petra explains that when the Blairs were here for the election there just wasn't room for everyone in the main house, it was crowded out, what with the cook and everyone. The cook? 'Well, she says, 'you wouldn't expect them to . . .'. Quite.

Cooks? Dressers? Armed guards to visit the village shop? Was it always like this? 'Not at all,' says Petra with relief, delighted to get on to the relatively safe topic of how things used to be when she and Cherie were young mothers together. 'We used to sit chatting in her kitchen. They have an Aga next door, you know.' I have read this before. The Aga was part of the fixtures and fittings when the Blairs took over the house.

'We would be in their kitchen chatting and Cherie would jump up and say, "I'll knock up a batch of cheese scones." And she would. She was good at cheese scones.' This hint that cooking is part of Cherie's repertoire doesn't really fit the image. She is also, according to Mrs Grieves, a canny shopper. Apparently Cherie was so keen on Ted Grieves' meat, and his out-of-London prices that when Tony went to the constituency alone Cherie would send him with a shopping list for the butcher. 'He used to take it back to London in his pockets,' said Petra.

Petra is a genuinely nice woman and obviously she has been close to Cherie. She seems really uncomfortable talking to me. She is absolutely terrified of doing anything which would upset Cherie. They have known one another for a very long time and she doesn't want to get into trouble.

It's difficult to make new friends if you are the Prime Minister's wife. However much you might like someone and enjoy their company it is hard to bring new people inside the circle. Are they to be trusted? Why do they want to be friends? There are very few people Cherie meets these days who wouldn't be flattered by an invitation to share a meal with the Blair family or an afternoon at the beauty salon with Cherie, but could it all end up on the front page of a national paper? Cherie might not react like this to the people she meets, but her protectors certainly do. There's always the unspoken question, what does this person want? Is there an underlying reason why this person wants to develop the relationship?

So the people closest to Cherie are her family. Tony, the children, her mum Gale, her sister Lyndsey, her cousin Kathryn Gray and people who work for the family. Ros Mark lived as part the Blair household and was absolutely trusted. That's why Cherie was so angry and upset when she found out that Ros had written a book about her life when she was living as part of the Blair family.

Just outside the family circle there are people Cherie feels she can trust just because she's known them for a long time. Her old school friend, Catherine Broadhurst, Leo's godmother is one. Cherie had been pleased to see her Seafield sewing teacher Sister Marie Clune again at a school reunion. Then there was a piece in a paper describing the Sister as a trusted adviser. 'Cherie consults her frequently', said the newspaper, and Downing Street issued a denial. Sister Marie was mortified and claimed she had been misquoted. She probably was. The nuns who used to run Seafield nowadays refuse to talk about Cherie to anyone at all.

Now that most of the Blair lives are spent in semi-public, family holidays have become precious oases in a desert of public appearances. Friends say that Cherie is always encouraging Tony to accept hospitality which brings with it privacy and luxury for a few weeks a year. She strongly believes they have earned it. But over the last few years the Blairs' luxury excursions have done more than anything else to shore up the image of a family out of touch with the real world who have come to expect a luxury lifestyle as part of the job. The Blairs' escapes to French chateaux and Italian palaces are often contrasted with the more modest holidays of other European leaders. When the Blairs were in Tuscany as the guests of the newspaper proprietor and law professor Prince Giraloma Strozzi at his hilltop Renaissance villa which has fifty rooms, a pool and secluded gardens, the German Chancellor Gerhard Schroeder and his wife were staying with their small daughter in a pension on the coast near Naples, which they paid for themselves. In summer 2001 while the Blairs were hidden from sight in a luxury Mexican resort, the Dutch Prime Minister Wim Kok and his wife were touring England in their Ford car and staying at bed and breakfast places. The Blair's exotic holidays have also included a villa near San Rossore in Tuscany which was loaned to them by the local government, an estate owned by the Premier of the Seychelles on the Indian ocean island of La Digue, and Sir David Keene's twelfth-century chateau in France. Cherie has enjoyed mini-breaks without Tony at Sir Cliff Richard's villa in the Algarve, and the British Ambassador's residence in Lisbon.

Cherie Booth is very much an urban creature. She was brought up in the big city. She went to university in London and she has spent all her working life here. Whatever else happens when Tony Blair stops being Prime Minister the Blairs will want to go back to living in London and that could present considerable problems. All Prime Ministers and their families feel isolated at the centre of their circle but the Blairs feel it more than most because Downing Street really is their home. They sold their house at 1 Richmond Crescent Islington within weeks of the 1997 election and they didn't buy another. Even Mrs Thatcher at the height of her power realized the vulnerability of not having a place she could escape to and bought the famous Barratt executive home in Dulwich, where she spent a few months when the Conservative Party got rid of her.

At the moment the Blairs seem very safe indeed in Downing Street, but not having somewhere to escape to, and not having a foot on the London housing ladder is the thing which worries Cherie most. She knows she and Tony made their biggest mistake when they sold Richmond Crescent so quickly. The Blairs were told that the house presented a security nightmare, and that it would cost more to make it safe for them than it was worth, so they sold it for £615,000 three months after the 1997 election. Four years on that amount of money would barely buy them a four-bedroom flat in central London. The Richmond Crescent house has been sold twice, the last time for £1.3 million. Mark Cullen who runs the Islington branch of Foxtons, the estate agents says: 'You'd think the Blairs, of all people, would have realized that house prices would shoot up under a Labour government!' According to him they really made a mess of things. Cherie spoke to the long-time local estate agents Holden Matthews and they thought she would instruct them to sell the house. But in the end she sold the house privately through a firm in Kensington. Cullen says he thinks she knew someone there and they sold the house to a French banker for quite a bit less than it was worth. The banker then spent £100,000 on his new property. He put in a new kitchen and bathroom and turned Richmond Crescent into an elegant and stylish house, then put it back on the market at £1.5 million: he accepted £1.3 million and sold it to professionals from the City. One hundred percent profit in four years. Cullen says it is going to cost the Blairs a lot of money to buy their way back into the London housing market. With Leo they will now need at least four and preferably five bedrooms if Gale is going to stay with them, or if they are going to continue to have a live-in nanny. 'Frankly,' he said, 'They are going to need over a million and a half pounds to buy a house like that. They'll need one of the big Georgian houses overlooking Highbury Fields, Highbury Place or Colebrook Row. You need big money to buy a place like that.'

To ordinary people in ordinary homes outside London these sound like fantasy figures, but people who live in London will understand. 'The key thing about London housing is that you must never take your foot off the ladder. That's what the Blairs did and it is going to be a hell of a job for them to get back on again. Really they need a deposit of over a million and a half pounds if they want to keep their mortgage down to a level that even a High Court Judge and an ex-Prime Minister could afford.' So Cherie Booth worries about where she and her family will live when their time at Downing Street comes to an end but she and her husband both know that if they start house hunting they will give an important signal to the nation that they've made their minds up about the future.

Fifteen
LOVE'S LAST WORD

Tony and Cherie have made it to the top. His ambition is
fulfilled. After four years as Britain's most popular Prime
Minister ever, he has won another election with a large majority
and secured another full term, the first ever Labour Prime
Minister to do so. Throughout he has been helped and
supported by his wife, who has successfully kept the flames
going under her own ambition without ever seeming to be in
competition with him. Publicly she has always backed and
supported him. Privately she has got on with what has always
been her personal aim, to advance the legal career she put on
the back burner for Tony. All those years of plodding up and
down to the constituency every weekend meant that she had to
ration the time she could spend on her legal work.

There were other unique achievements for the Blairs during
the fourth Labour Government. They added another child to
their family – Leo, the first baby born in Downing Street for 150
years. Cherie is the first ever Prime Minister's wife to work at
her profession while living in Downing Street, and she successfully defended clients in the courts who were fighting against her
husband's Government.

During their time at the top the Prime Minister has aged
visibly. His hair is thinning and greying, he can look irritable and
seem tired and tetchy. Often during the 2001 election campaign
he seemed out of touch with the voters he met, unsure of what
to say to them. The electorate seemed to disappoint him, as if it
had failed to live up to his expectations.

Cherie on the other hand has grown in strength and confidence.

Her hair is glossy, her eyes shine, her skin glows. On a post-election visit to Mexico she was photographed soaking wet and glistening with glamour at the Iguazu Falls. Happy and confident, she looked ready to take on all comers.

In public the Blairs are very disciplined. When there are cameras present, and there usually are because their access is restricted and cameramen must seize every opportunity, the Blairs do only what has been agreed in advance with their media minders. They rarely go off script or make a chance remark and there's no access to Cherie. On the only occasions where Cherie has made off-the-cuff comments, they have seemed tasteless and out of character for 'Mrs Blair'. At the Labour Party conference in 1999 she was shown the Viagra stall. 'We don't need that,' she remarked. In the 2001 election campaign she was asked to pose for a photograph with Tony on the Prime Ministerial plane. 'Are you trying to make us look as if we have joined the Mile High Club?' she joked.

In January 2000 Cherie was forced to speak up for herself. On her first day as a Crown Court Recorder she failed to buy a ticket for the rail journey from Blackfriars in London to Luton and was given an on-the-spot fine of ten pounds. The next day, defiantly clutching a ticket for her journey, she was asked by the press if the incident had been an embarassment for her. She replied: 'Certainly was!'

The Blairs and their media minders work together with sympathetic journalists to make sure all coverage is favourable. More humble politicians who have no control over the press (and no prizes to offer) have to be satisfied with the coverage that's meted out to them. Journalists and others who step out of line with the Blairs are disciplined rigorously. Most who work in the parliamentary lobby are fearful of shouting questions or doing anything the Blairs won't like because they know it will mean they will put future access in jeopardy. The Blairs know just how competitive the media are for stories about them, and they hand out their favours carefully. They know that news organizations are going to be extremely reluctant to put their access to the Prime Minister and his wife at risk. Tony and Cherie Blair are the most powerful couple in Britain. With that power comes the control that they exercise over the media.

Inside the stockade there is a remarkable set of interlocking partnerships. Tony Blair and Alastair Campbell have worked closely together in the last seven years as a real team. Fiona Millar works equally diligently on Mrs Blair's behalf.

Mrs Blair grants access only for photo opportunities, and woe betide the occasional happy snapper. Hers is still mostly a non-speaking role and it seems overall to have been a successful strategy. Cherie's time as Mrs Blair has been largely gaffe-free, perhaps partly due to the terror her powerful media team can strike in journalists: access can be denied at any moment and for any reason, with privacy cited as an excuse. There is a strict understanding that no questions are to be asked, and if the Millar-controlled routine is in any way disrupted there will be no future access for the journalists concerned.

Nicholas Jones summarizes how this control is wielded: 'I've been at a number of occasions where Cherie has been with Fiona and Fiona would stand slightly to one side, and she's really watching like a hawk to see what the news media are doing. She's keeping one eye on Cherie, she's keeping one eye on us. And I would know she wouldn't look at me, she wouldn't engage me in conversation, but she's keeping an eye on what I'm doing, and if I broke the rules, if I moved forward, tried to jump Mrs Blair and ask her a question, well, that would be curtains: I'd get into trouble, deep trouble.'

This strict management has left many other women in public

life envious. Cherie is protected because she is the Prime
Minister's wife and she is able to use that protected position
inside the Blair laager to improve her own career prospects. No
one questions the fact that Cherie Booth is a top barrister with
a promising future. But because she is the Prime Minister's wife
she gets off so much more lightly than other women who are
thrown into the public spotlight.

The Blairs' control of a managed press has been so successful
that very little has emerged over the past seven years about the
relationships between those inside the Blair stockade. Nobody
asks questions about the relationships the Prime Minister and
his wife have with Campbell and Millar. Yet both Campbell and
Millar have the status of civil servants and are publicly accountable.

Of course the Blairs are not the first Downing Street residents
to protect their privacy. But in the past, the media pressure to
tell everything to everyone did not exist, and personal lives were
off limits unless they reached the courts. There are plenty of
examples in the past of journalists knowing what was going on
in Downing Street but not revealing a word of it in their papers,
because in previous ages the charmed circle saw it as part of
their job not to tell the people. Prime Minister Lloyd George
had an affair for many years with his secretary Frances
Stevenson in Downing Street itself, while his wife stayed in his
constituency in North Wales. Westminster journalists were all
aware of the situation. Nothing was reported. Lady Dorothy
Macmillan, wife of Prime Minister Harold Macmillan, had a
long affair with Robert Boothby while she was living in
Downing Street but Macmillan ignored the situation: indeed,
such was his magnanimity that he made Boothby a peer. The
press knew what was going on but regarded it as their duty to
keep quiet.

Yet we are now in the early years of the twenty-first century. The second term of the Blair Government has begun and it seems that there will be no relaxation of a successful policy of news management. The same tough rules which proved so successful for the Blairs in the beginning are still firmly in place.

The Blairs' privacy is protected so obsessively because they and their protectors want at all times to demonstrate that they are in control. They'll dole out the human touches, the little glimpses of endearing gems of family life, but they won't allow anything else to be prized out by anyone. The leader and his wife and family will be protected at all costs against the intrusion of journalists into their private world.

So why is this control so important? Tony Blair doesn't have a mistress on the premises, or anywhere else – preachy-teachy not rumpy-pumpy is his style. Cherie is not involved in a relationship with someone in the House of Lords. The Blairs are well known to be a genuinely happy family: devout, serious, getting on with their work, bringing up their children in a way that they ask us to admire at election time. Are they trying to hide the fact that Cherie is untidy and her kitchen is a mess?

Those of us in the Westminster village know that Tony and Cherie bicker and scrap just like most happily married couples. We even know that Tony has some characteristics that would make him the object of admiration, especially for tired young mums struggling with jobs, kids and uncooperative husbands. He really is a modern father who believes in equality and sharing the load of family responsibilities with his wife. When he has told us that he's the one who changes nappies in the middle of the night, that Cherie might sleep on while he attends to baby Leo, he really is telling it how it is – much to the disgust of Alastair Campbell, who doesn't hold with world leaders taking their family responsibilities quite so seriously, and to the surprise of many visitors including Nelson Mandela. There were several rows about the Prime Minister's underperformance around the time of Blair's disastrous slow-handclapped speech to the Women's Institute conference at Wembley in June 2000, a month after Leo's birth. Campbell tried unsuccessfully to get Blair to get more rest, yet Blair puts fatherhood before everything else. He ignored Campbell completely. The public saw how tired the Prime Minister was and how he underperformed for the six months following the birth of Leo. Should he have concentrated on running the country? Campbell thought so, and it's a legitimate question, but one the Prime Minister doesn't want to have to answer.

But what of Cherie? There is no doubt that she blossomed and seemed to gain in confidence with the birth of Leo. We all admired her because within weeks she was back at work. But within weeks Cherie was also back to playing the part of the silent spouse, 'Mrs Cherie Blair' the dutiful wife, accompanying her husband at times when he wanted her support, demonstrating over and over again that this silent support was correct behaviour for the wife of the Prime Minister.

It's time for a change.

There is no doubt that inside the family Cherie is the boss. Just like other strong Liverpool women before her, she is the heart of her family and assumes the role of the boss quite naturally. I asked Blair's Sedgefield agent John Burton why Cherie was so silent when she was at Tony's side in public and he gave an interesting answer: 'I think that's her choice. I think the reason she is so silent during elections, it is a bit like the quiz games, she wants to give Tony his chance to shine. She doesn't want to be seen as speaking out on his behalf, She lets him do that.'

Surely now that she has shown how well she can do the silent adoration and the clever career woman routines, and blossom at both, the time has come to get rid of 'Mrs Cherie Blair'. It's time for the real Cherie Booth to step forward and the world to be allowed to see the Blairs as they really are – a modern couple who are truly equal, supportive to one another but with two separate careers on twin tracks running, so far, side by side. It is time that we had a better and more truthful role model for women to aspire to. Cherie is named as the most powerful woman in Britain, the most influential, but this cannot be because she is so successful at standing silently at her husband's side. People think she is powerful and influential because they don't believe the public image, because they think there is something else about Cherie which is hidden from view.

Of course Cherie Booth has every right to turn down the offer of a real role in British public life. I have always judged that she is a feminist who believes in equality and wants to see other women have the same opportunities that she has enjoyed. But maybe her other role as a Catholic mother of a large family and her husband's wife is what she really values. We simply don't know. We assume that she is a feminist who wants to advance the position of women in society, but it could be that her ambition is limited to her own position. We talk of her as a role model, as someone who goes out to work and brings up her family successfully. We suspect that she wants to promote a better deal for women because she argues for paternity leave for men and worries about the difficulties for young women barristers, yet we know nothing, because the public part of Mrs Cherie Booth, the smiling icon at her husband's side, is in such direct conflict with the lives ordinary women have to live and the work they are expected to do.

Cherie Booth has a perfect opportunity over the next four

years to throw away the empty shell which is 'Mrs Blair' and which has begun to evoke comparisons with the behaviour of Princes Diana. Cherie Booth as the Prime Minister's wife has the opportunity to play a really useful part in the liberalization of British society and to start campaigning for some real equality for women. There is no danger to her husband's government with its solid majority. The worst that might happen is that a few old misogynists will write articles complaining that the Prime Minister's wife has no right to interfere in politics or to broadcast her own opinions, yet such would be drowned in waves of support and approval from ordinary women who would be delighted at the idea of someone with acknowledged power and influence speaking out on their behalf. If Cherie Booth was to make it clear that she was a real supporter of equality for women and not just paying lip service like so many of the ministers in her husband's government, it could make a huge difference.

It is not only women who need to see a change in Cherie. If we are to get anywhere near to promoting an equal society, men as well as women need to be educated about the ways they should behave towards their working wives, if the kind of equal society the Blair Government says it is promoting is to have a chance of success. There has never been a better opportunity for a Prime Minister's wife to take a brave course and say what she really means. We have come a long way since the 1960s when Jackie Kennedy, having been asked a political question, sighed and giggled breathily: 'You'll have to ask Jack that one'. Yet that metaphorically is what 'Mrs Blair' is doing. Cherie Booth does not have to go on playing the part of Mrs Blair. If she wants to help women she has every right to use her powerful role to do so. No one would have argued that Denis Thatcher didn't have a right to his opinions just because he was married to the Prime Minister. Because Cherie goes on with such determination playing the part of the dominated wife, the opportunity for real action is beginning to melt away.

Cherie Both personally has more choices to make. She is an extremely persuasive and powerful woman. She has always had an equal relationship with her husband Tony, and even while he has been Prime Minister she has made sure that they have shared domestic roles equally. It has emerged clearly that it's Tony rather than Cherie who puts the family first at all times. It seems clear that Cherie has definite future career plans which involve her taking a leading legal role in British society while her husband adjusts his ambitions to suit. Perhaps it is perceived in the family that he has had his turn at the top, his moment in the sun and mum's is yet to come. The Blairs will be thinking carefully about his future in the way they calculate so much else, so the intermittent hints that Tony really wants to spend more time with his family and give Cherie the opportunity to develop her career may well represent an emerging reality.

Cherie could play a vital public political role if she was to throw away the carapace of Mrs Blair which she wears for protection on wifely public occasions and take up a leading role as campaigner for equality in family life. That's unlikely. While she is prepared to pay lip service to equality of the sexes, it is her own career as a barrister that she has concentrated on for the last twenty-five years. Cherie Booth is just as ambitious as the next QC. There is nothing to stop her becoming a High Court Judge. She is on her way as an Assistant Recorder. The top of the tree for anyone in Cherie's position is of course the job of Lord Chancellor.

She has shown she is determined to keep her job, and she will not stay where she is. She might be Lord Chancellor some day.

I asked John Burton how long he thought the Blairs would stay on at Number 10. 'We have never talked about it, but I would be disappointed if he doesn't stay on. I would like to see him continue. If he went for the third term that would be it. I don't think he could be Prime Minister any longer than that. I think it is such a huge job and more than three terms would be far too long. Cherie's still got plenty of time to achieve things after that!'

A woman who was at school with her remembered Cherie dreaming of being Britain's first ever female Prime Minister. That opportunity was snapped up by Margaret Thatcher in 1979, but the law has never had a female leader. What more suitable climax to the career of the ambitious Cherie than the Lord Chancellor's job? The Blairs' oldest and dearest friend Derry Irvine has been Lord Chancellor throughout Tony Blair's leadership, and Cherie will certainly be on the list of eager contenders to inherit his robes. Who isn't attracted to the idea of Chancellor Cherie, hair glossy, eyes shining, sailing through Westminster in her Chancellor's robes while her husband Tony takes a more back-seat role educating Leo in the finer points of football in the park?

There is of course the obvious question of whether Cherie Booth is suited to a high profile public role where she has to be accountable for her own actions rather than remain silent about her husband's? It is hard to know. Her obsession with secrecy suggests that she may find it difficult but she seems to want to try, and a legal judicial role is very different from the hurly-burly of a politician's. Cherie has all the qualifications and has worked hard at the remoteness.

The man who must be watching her bid for the top most carefully is next door neighbour Gordon Brown. Brown knows what a powerful woman Cherie is. He knows too that in the end it will be her decision rather than the Prime Minister's whether Tony stays at the end of his second term. If Brown is to have a chance to be the next leader of the Labour Party he needs an early departure and an endorsement from Tony Blair. He therefore needs Cherie to make her mind up to go for the legal top.

The idea of Prime Minister Gordon Brown appointing the first female Lord Chancellor certainly sounds plausible.

Whatever happens in the future there is no doubt at all that Cherie Booth has been the most interesting person ever to have played the part of consort at Downing Street. The fact that she has not been able to push her childhood experiences aside and has felt she has had to hide away so much from the public gaze has been her millstone. The fact that she has been unwilling to reveal what a strong and effective woman she is, living in an equal marriage with the most powerful man in the land, is our loss. If only Cherie had been able to demonstrate publicly that women and men can achieve real equality in their marriages and their careers irrespective of their position in society, she could have made an important contribution to the advancement of women in Britain. It is time for her to begin.

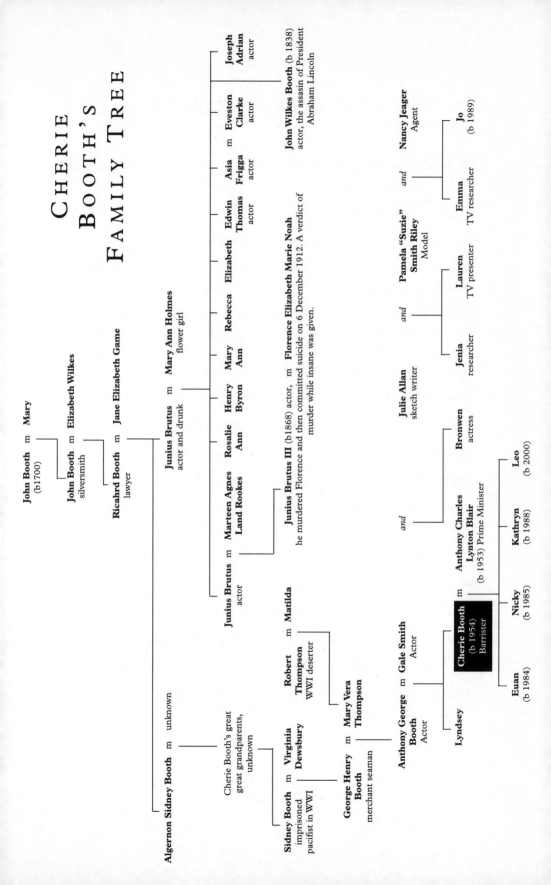

CHERIE
BOOTH'S
FAMILY TREE

John Booth m **Mary**
(b1700)

John Booth m **Elizabeth Wilkes**
silversmith

Richahrd Booth m **Jane Elizabeth Game**
lawyer

Junius Brutus m **Mary Ann Holmes**
actor and drunk   flower girl

Joseph Adrian
actor

Elizabeth   **Asia Frigga** m **Eveston Clarke**
                 actor   actor

Edwin Thomas
actor

Rebecca   **Mary Ann**   **Henry Byron**   **Rosalie Ann**

John Wilkes Booth (b 1838)
actor, the assasin of President
Abraham Lincoln

Junius Brutus m **Marteen Agnes Land Rookes**
actor

Junius Brutus III (b1868) actor, m **Florence Elizabeth Marie Noah**
he murdered Florence and then committed suicide on 6 December 1912. A verdict of
murder while insane was given.

Algernon Sidney Booth m unknown

Cherie Booth's great
great grandparents,
unknown

Sidney Booth m **Virginia Dewsbury**
imprisoned
pacifist in WWI

Robert Thompson m **Matilda**
WWI deserter

George Henry Booth m **Mary Vera Thompson**
merchant seaman

Anthony George Booth m **Gale Smith**
Actor   Actor

Julie Allan
sketch writer

and

Anthony Charles Lynton Blair
(b 1953) Prime Minister

Bronwen
actress

Pamela "Suzie" Smith Riley
Model

Nancy Jeager
Agent

m

Cherie Booth
(b 1954)
Barrister

Jenia
researcher

and

Lauren
TV presenter

and

Emma
TV researcher

Jo
(b 1989)

Lyndsey

Euan
(b 1984)

Nicky
(b 1985)

Kathryn
(b 1988)

Leo
(b 2000)

Bibliography

Paddy Ashdown, *The Ashdown Diaries, Volume 1: 1988 to 1997* (Allen Lane/ The Penguin Press 2000)

Beatles Anthology (Cassell 2000)

Tony Booth *Stroll On: an autobiography* (Sidgwick and Jackson 1989)

Colin Brown *Fighting Talk: the Biography of John Prescott* (Simon & Schuster 1997)

Michael Brunson *A Ringside Seat* (Hodder & Stoughton 2000)

David Butler and Gareth Butler *British Political Facts* (Macmillan 2000)

Edwina Currie *She's Leaving Home* (Little Brown 1997)

Bryan Gould *Goodbye to All That* (Macmillan 1995)

David Hare *Asking Around* (Faber and Faber 1993)

Peter Hennessy *The Prime Minister* (Allen Lane/Penguin Press 2000)

Nicholas Jones *Sultans of Spin* (Victor Gollancz 1999)

Peter Oborne *Alastair Campbell: New Labour and the rise of the media class* (Aurum Press 1999)

Andrew Rawnsley *Servants of the People* (Hamish Hamilton 2000)

John Rentoul *Tony Blair* (Little Brown 1995)

John Rentoul *Tony Blair, Prime Minister* (Little Brown 2001)

Geoffrey Robinson *The Unconventional Minister* (Michael Joseph 2000)

Paul Routledge *Gordon Brown: the biography* (Simon & Schuster 1998)

Paul Routledge *Mandy: the unauthorized biography of Peter Mandelson* (Simon & Schuster 1999)

Index